HE KNOWS *Your* NAME

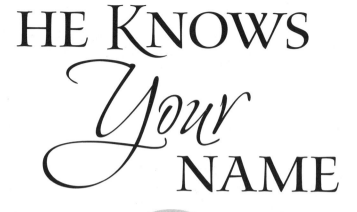

HOW ONE ABANDONED BABY INSPIRED ME TO SAY YES TO GOD

LINDA ZNACHKO

with MARGOT STARBUCK

Debbie -

Be inspired to say Yes!

Kregel
Publications

To Steven.
Your generosity and sweet love have been the wind
beneath my wings. Being your bride is my joy.

To my precious children,
Lauren, Andrew, Anna, and Caroline.
When I birthed you, you gave me life.

For your beautiful name, Jesus.
I humbly lay this all down at your feet.

CONTENTS

INTRODUCTION

I have enjoyed a privileged life.

I was raised in a loving family and now have one of my own: an adoring husband, four children, two of whom are married, and I am over the moon enjoying my first grandchild. My husband runs a successful business. We live in a beautiful home, we have been to some of the most exotic places in the world, and we can afford to send our kids to college.

Privilege, though, doesn't exempt anyone from the bumps and bruises of life. The difficulties each of us face know no boundaries of geography, race, age, or income. Whether it's the loss of a child, the end of a marriage, chronic health issues, the death of a dream—pain comes to us all.

This story is born out of one of those painful seasons. My mother was facing terminal cancer and my daughter was battling the uncertainty of debilitating disease. My husband and I were forced to leave our precious daughter at a treatment center a thousand miles from our home, begging God that this painful decision would somehow save our daughter's life. The agony of the impending loss of my mother and the possible loss of my daughter crushed me. When we left the facility and stopped for gas, I began screaming hysterically, swearing at my husband, accusing him, and demanding, "We have to go back! We can't leave our daughter!" Steve, with tears running down his cheeks, chest heaving, grabbed me and held me tight as we stood in the pouring rain. Unable to move, we gripped each other so we would not fall. We had come completely undone.

In that most difficult season, when I felt torn daily between being at my mother's bedside and being where I could best support my daughter, all I wanted to do was to erect boundaries, hide behind barriers, hunker down, and fight for the life of my child and for my family. But God had a very different plan. Not only would God deny me permission to set up new boundaries, he was about to tear down *all* my existing ones.

After my mother died and my daughter returned to a normal school routine, an unlikely journey with God began when I learned about a baby whose body had been found in an urban dumpster. The naive, hesitant yes I offered to God's prompting that day would launch the most unlikely journey. How could I ever have imagined that, at the moment I wanted to run from my own pain, God would heal me by sending me to help carry the pain of others? How could I have known that life's meaning would be revealed so vividly in places of death? The assurance that "God's ways are not our ways" took on unexpected meaning and, ultimately, it was *his* way, not mine, that brought me back to life.

My natural impulse was to avoid suffering. To push away pain. To dodge death. I shied away from what was uncomfortable. Awkward. Unpredictable. I wanted comfort and I sought that comfort in all kinds of ways: I read the latest Christian best sellers, I was active in several Bible studies, I attended women's conferences, I planned family vacations—but those distractions could not keep my pain and sadness at bay.

As I accepted Jesus's invitation to go where he was leading, I experienced my own comfort among those who suffer: the grieving widow, the childless parent, the abandoned spouse, the suffering survivor. When I followed Jesus, often with uncertainty, he led me into the sacred place of suffering where I found the strength and comfort I was looking for. It's where I found new life. And though I still don't presume to know what God is up to, I can say for certain that every time I have squeaked out another hesitant yes, God has led the way and God's presence has been enough.

Because human suffering is *where he is*, as God binds up the wounds of the brokenhearted (Psalm 147:3), it's also the surprising place at which

I encountered grace and was transformed. It's where God continues to meet me today, and I'm convinced that—however suffering touches your life or the lives of those around you—it's where God longs to meet you.

—Linda Znachko

"Baby Found in Dumpster"

"Breaking News: Baby Found in Dumpster."

I sat dumbfounded in front of my computer, struggling to make sense of the words scrolling across the online news site. I'd just come inside from the crisp October chill and shuddered at the thought of a child having been abandoned to the elements to die.

"Baby Doe wearing only a diaper."

The words seemed like nonsense, and I was unable to process them. Other words settled into my heart:

Doe is not a name.
A dumpster is not a grave.
A diaper is not burial clothing.

The video accompanying the news story showed police investigating the industrial dumpster where a couple, searching for scrap metal, had found a baby's body earlier in the day. The masks worn by the gloved professionals weren't enough to disguise the sadness on their faces. A twisting blue light flashed above a squad car. Yellow caution tape stretched across the downtown parking lot, keeping curious onlookers from getting in the way.

What I was feeling, however, was far more than curiosity. As my heart began to quicken I recognized the nudge of the Holy Spirit, prompting me to act. God had been training me for years to follow in faith by taking one small step at a time. Although I could never predict what God had in store, I knew God was now inviting me to say yes to the Spirit's unlikely leading.

Quickly scanning for the byline, I called the *Indianapolis Star* and asked for the journalist who'd reported the story: John Touhy. Perhaps he'd be able to answer my questions.

When he picked up the call, I introduced myself and asked for his help.

"So, what happens to this baby?" I pressed.

In a gravelly voice, he patiently explained that the investigation was now a legal matter.

"The only one who can answer your questions," he explained, "is the coroner. I'm waiting to hear back from her office right now—Chief Deputy Ballew."

"I'll try her. Thank you so much for your help," I said before hanging up.

Knowing city offices had closed for the night, I would call the next day.

BEDTIME MUSINGS

After I had spoken to John Touhy, I explained my strange attachment to this child to my husband, Steve. Though neither one of us could have predicted the absurd unfolding of the day's events, Steve had always been the person in my life who was more afraid of saying no to God than of agreeing to even the most complicated or unwieldy yes. So, although we had no idea how this child would continue to impact our lives, Steve was quick to lend his support and encouragement.

When I climbed into bed that night, slipping between smooth satin sheets, thoughts of the precious little one continued to pulse through my heart and mind. The words that had so gripped me when I read the jarring news headline still rang in my ears: *A dumpster is not a grave.*

Grabbing my thick, blue, spiral-bound journal from my nightstand, I scribbled down the facts, writing what I knew as if to try to understand what I did not.

No name.
No funeral.
No burial clothes.
No songs.
No readings.
No blessing to acknowledge that this child *did* live.

As precious memories from my mother's funeral, just four months earlier, flooded my mind, I felt as though I was reeling in some alternate universe. The gruesome end of this child's earthly days suggested that he or she had never lived. But, I insisted to myself, this child *had* lived. If only growing inside a mother's womb. This baby *lived*.

Pressing pen to paper, I continued to process:

> A child of God was left to die in a dumpster. He or she was found early Wednesday morning by a couple looking for scrap metal. Looking for scrap, they found the remains of a baby. Buried in a trash heap.

Life and death had been close to my heart over the course of the year. My daughter's fragile health hung in the balance. At that moment, we didn't yet know if she would live. And although cancer had ravaged my mother's body, it had not stolen her dignity. I continued to contrast the lavish funeral she'd received, honoring the inestimable value of her life, with the crude treatment of this precious little one.

"This baby needs a name," I wrote. "God already knows it because it is, after all, written in the book of life. We just don't know it yet. But he or she has one, and deserves one."

FURTHER DIGGING

The next morning, I waited until just after nine to call the Marion County Coroner's Office. An administrative assistant fielded some of my questions.

"The body will be disposed of after the case is closed," she explained. Her language shocked me. Garbage is disposed of. Babies are not.

"What does 'disposed of' mean?" I asked, trying to quell in my voice the rage and sadness I felt inside.

"It means a pauper's grave . . . a mass grave," she told me.

A jolt of indignation shot through my body. *What?*

Now my head was spinning.

In 2009? I'd never imagined such a thing existed right where I live.

I silently vowed, *No way. Not if I can do anything about it.*

The receptionist told me I'd need to call back later to reach the coroner. So I called throughout the morning until I was able to speak to Chief Deputy Ballew. I explained my intentions, that I was interested in giving the baby a proper burial. She confessed that she'd never received a call like mine before.

"I'd like to be granted the legal *right* to the child," I pressed.

"Well . . ." She paused, thinking through my last comment. "I can put your name and number in the file. That way I can call you when the criminal investigation is completed and the case is officially closed."

The situation was highly unusual and I could tell that Alfarena Ballew was trying to honor my request while upholding the law and doing her job with integrity.

"Promise me," I begged, "that you will."

She promised.

In the quiet of my heart, as I hung up the phone, I prayed that God would allow me the privilege to do what my heart was aching and longing to do by honoring and dignifying the life of this child.

PURSUING A PROPER BURIAL

Every Friday, I called Alfie's office, hoping for a crack in the case. Perhaps there would be some new lead. A shred of evidence. I waited eagerly, hoping this little one would be released into my care.

As the case unfolded in the media, a barrage of local news reports painted a picture of an unknown, heartless mother who disposed of an unwanted child in this callous manner. At night I continued to journal:

> I can't get this mother off my mind. Every day I think about her. I woke up today thinking about how adorable Andrew, my

son, was at three months. Chubbiness sets in. Smiles come and babies are sleeping through the night at that age. I *wanted* my son. I don't know if anyone ever wanted Baby Doe. Probably not.

As I wrestled to assemble these disparate pieces into a comprehensible whole, I could only imagine that this baby was unwanted. I continued to reflect in my journal:

> Being wanted changes everything in the heart of a child or an adult's life. I see it so often in friends and family members of mine. To be welcomed, adored, and desired versus being an intrusion, an interruption, or a disappointment. We all feel it deeply and it somewhat defines us deep down.

Alfie warned me that a criminal investigation could become quite lengthy—quite unlike the ones solved in sixty minutes on television. This provided plenty of time for the what-if questions, about all I didn't understand and couldn't control, to creep into my mind, tempting me to stray from obedience. But, reminding me that I didn't need to see the future he already saw, God was teaching me to trust him one step at a time: all I needed to do was to walk through the door in front of me. So God gave me small steps to accomplish as I waited to discover the identity of this baby: I called a funeral home to arrange a service; I contacted a cemetery that had served other abandoned babies; I prayed for the woman who'd given birth to the baby found in the dumpster.

All I knew about the baby's mother was what I'd gleaned from TV. I had no way of knowing whether or not she was the monster others imagined when they watched the evening news. I didn't know if she'd wanted her child or wanted to get rid of him or her. My instinct told me that whether her child had been planned or unplanned, she would still be grieving. My only certainty was that, whoever she was, God loved her and was filled with overwhelming compassion for her. During the months of waiting, as God continued to soften my heart for this mother, I continued to pour out my thoughts in the pages of my journal:

Baby Doe has a name; I just don't know it yet. I will meet a grieving mother. I will offer her help. I will tell her she has not been alone this past year. I have waited with her. I have hoped with her that this baby would be given dignity.

And I prayed that God would open a door for me to know her.

I suspect my heart connected so deeply with this mother because I too was grieving—as a mother and as a daughter. I was a grieving daughter, having recently buried my mother. But I was also a mother who was grieving the precarious future of the daughter I loved.

Anna's terrifying illness, which could easily have snatched her away from our family, had activated both my fierce maternal instincts to protect her and a fiery advocacy on her behalf before the throne of God. These same impulses were unleashed again when this baby's body was discovered in a dumpster. And they fueled me as I fought to honor the life of that child as if he or she were my own.

How many times had I watched the horrors on the evening news, breathed a quiet prayer for those who suffered, and returned to my life and family? And yet now God's Spirit was prompting me to step into a stranger's deepest pain. Had I declined, no one around me would have been the wiser. Had I heeded the internal voice reminding me how awkward it was to be pursuing something that wasn't my business or my area of expertise, my life would have continued as it was, normal but lacking and slightly broken. But somehow my small yes to making one phone call was opening me up to sense and respond to God's leading in a fresh new way. Calling me into deeper obedience, God daily assured my heart—in the time we spent together each morning—that his voice was the only one that mattered.

CHAPTER 2

Though My Father and
Mother Forsake Me

On a crisp, cold January morning, just three months after learning of the baby who had been abandoned, I dropped my husband off at the Indianapolis International Airport for a men's leadership retreat in Florida. Returning home, I felt the bite of bitter cold in my garage, and perhaps a nip of jealousy that I wasn't headed to Florida. I ducked into the house and went upstairs to my desk.

Since it was a Friday, I did what I did every Friday morning: I called the coroner's office to check on the Baby Doe investigation. As had been the case every Friday for the last three months, Alfie relayed that there were no new developments.

"But," she added with a long pause, "I'm glad you called. I was just about to call you."

Call me with no news? She piqued my curiosity.

Alfie went on to tell me about a baby who had been abandoned at the coroner's office. A five-month-old, African-American male, who had died of natural causes while at his grandmother's home. Since there was no criminal investigation into the circumstances surrounding the death, the baby's body could be released.

For one month, however, no one had claimed him.

The more Alfie shared, the more troubled I felt.

And as she spoke, I glanced through the sunroom and noticed my dog, Sedalia, a yellow lab, frolicking in the back yard. If I *had* been able to join Steve on his trip to Florida, we would have dropped Sedalia at a local kennel the previous day. In order to leave her for even a long week-end, we would have been obligated to sign a document acknowledging that abandoning a dog at a kennel was a criminal violation. We would even be bound to pay all legal fees if prosecution became necessary! And yet a child wasn't afforded the same protection?

My head swirled with more questions, and each answer Alfie shared broke my heart.

Neither the boy's mother, who was homeless, nor her family had taken any steps to accept responsibility for him. They wouldn't even respond to the coroner's request to retrieve him for burial. Though the chief investigator for the case had visited the home of the baby's grandmother and made repeated phone calls, the family had ignored the requests.

As Alfie spoke, I was already feeling a familiar internal tug to embrace this child by giving him a dignified burial. Then Alfie asked me if my "organization" would want to help.

Thankfully, I didn't blurt out what I was thinking: *What organization? Did I need one?*

While others would begin to catch the vision for life that God was sowing in my heart, and would eventually ask to join in, at that point there wasn't any *organization*. There was simply the gentle whisper of God's voice, "This baby needs a family and I'm in this with you. I am all you need."

I certainly didn't feel equipped for what lay ahead. *Who in their right mind*, I wondered, *would willingly move toward death instead of flee from it?* No sooner had I wondered it than a face filled my mind. It was the countenance of Jesus who, moved by love, had chosen the sting of death.

At least I was in good company.

For years I had been growing to recognize the sound of God's voice, even when he asked the most unlikely things, and I knew beyond a shadow of a doubt that I had been called to do this.

That was enough.

A few years earlier I had been given Mother Teresa's book *No Greater Love* as a gift. In it she writes, "I will take any child, any time, night or day. Just let me know and I will come for him."[1] I felt this same sense of urgency about Zachary.

LOOSE ENDS

Alfie patiently detailed some of the obstacles surrounding the case.

Because the baby's mother didn't have a residence, she wouldn't be able to request assistance from the Marion County Trustee office that offered a small stipend toward burial to struggling families. Cremation, Alfie explained, would be the cheapest option. She told me that Derek Harris, the coroner assigned to Zachary's case, had located the mother in the community just two days prior. Alfie read bits from his report to me that noted that the mother had been "dismissive in attitude" about her child. The baby's mother, she explained, had washed her hands of all responsibility for burial.

A flash of rage at a mother I did not know surged through my body and a single thought pounded in my mind: *I don't understand her.*

The voice inside me was answered by a gentler, kinder voice: *"Right. You can't and you never will."*

Humility seeped into my heart that had so suddenly been seized by anger and judgment. I didn't know this woman. I couldn't comprehend what she'd endured in her past; I didn't understand her pain; I could not fathom her hopelessness. As a person with resources—not just financial, but social and emotional and spiritual—I had no idea what it was like to live in her skin, to see the world through her eyes.

And in that moment God's Spirit replaced my judgment with a confidence in his love for her. Although I might not ever fully understand her, God knew her name and he loved her. In the same way I held my children in my heart, this woman was held in the heart of God.

She, too, had been somebody's baby.

Before I would get more deeply involved, however, I still wanted to make sure that this mother understood that there *could* be resources available to her. I wondered if access to resources to honor her son's life might equip her to engage as a mother. I wouldn't usurp that from her, if she would respond.

As we were hanging up, Alfie connected me to Derek Harris. Explaining who I was, I asked for his help.

I explained that I wanted to bury this baby boy and asked him if he would be willing to approach the baby's mother one more time. Because he needed to have her consent for burial, he was willing. He offered to return to the homeless community to find her.

"First," I requested, "can you make sure that she knows she will have help if she wants to bury her baby? I want her to have that option."

"Yes," he agreed. "I can explain that to her."

But we both knew how his first visit had gone. Though neither of us spoke it, we knew that this desperate mother might still balk.

"And if not," I continued, "can you ask her to sign away her rights so that he can be released to me? I want her to make an informed choice, but if she refuses to care for him, I want to be able to adopt him freely."

As I spoke the word "adopt," a deep resolve rippled through my frame to claim this precious child as my own, with the same steadfast faithful love that God had extended to me. The same love God had for this baby's mother.

BABY ZACHARY

Years ago, when I was pregnant with my second child, I sensed in my spirit that I was going to have a boy. I loved the name Zachary. But the two "Z's"—Zachary Znachko—just seemed a bit too much. So when my son arrived we named him Andrew Steven.

Alfie had told me that the name of this unclaimed child was Zachary. As I held him in my heart, I experienced clarity that *this* was the Zachary God had planted in my heart years earlier. This baby was God's idea, and if he remained unclaimed, I would add him to my family like my own.

Whether he would be buried by his first mother or by me, I knew I needed to find a cemetery. As sunlight streamed through my office window, I combed through archives of news stories about other babies who had been abandoned.

As I searched, I discovered one ministry near Chicago called Rest in

His Arms. There, a woman named Susan Walker had been traveling a path similar to the one down which the Lord seemed to be leading me. Passionate that every life matters, she had been providing Christian funerals and burials for babies who had been abandoned.

I wasn't alone.

I emailed Susan, who kindly pointed me toward resources for the journey. One in particular caught my attention. So before I even knew exactly what Zachary's future might hold, I placed an order for something special I hoped would honor him.

Continuing my local online search, I learned that two Indianapolis children who had been abandoned in recent years had been buried at Washington Park East.

I dialed the cemetery and waited, wondering whether anyone there would be willing to help me. When a sensitive, sweet voice answered the phone, I knew I'd found my helper. After I explained the unusual situation, the kind woman assured me she would go straight to the cemetery's manager with my need. True to her word, my phone rang before the end of the business day to schedule an appointment with the funeral home and secure a cemetery plot.

I'll keep moving ahead, I decided, *no matter who finally lays this infant to rest.*

The next day, as I finished up my lunch in the kitchen, my phone rang. I recognized the number of the coroner's office.

"Hello?" I answered quickly, eager to know what was happening.

"Mrs. Znachko, this is Derek Harris. I visited the mother of Zachary Tibbetts and she signed over her rights."

I hadn't expected to hear back from him so quickly.

"Did she hesitate?" I queried. "Did she want to bury him?"

"No." He sighed. I thought I heard an apologetic tone in his voice, as if he might have garnered a different response if he'd tried harder. Or perhaps what I heard was an acknowledgment of what felt, to both of us, shameful. He added, "She was ready to be done. The baby is yours."

"Thank you," I gasped.

Zachary was now mine.

After Coroner Harris explained the procedures I needed to follow and the paperwork to be done, we hung up.

Though the kitchen was silent, my heart and mind were busy, searching for answers.

Words from Isaiah filled my spirit:

> Can a mother forget the baby at her breast
>> and have no compassion on the child she has borne?
> Though she may forget,
>> I will not forget you!
> See, I have engraved you on the palms of my hands;
>> your walls are ever before me.
>
> (Isaiah 49:15–16)

I understood that, for reasons that were complicated, Zachary's mother wasn't able to care for him. Yet I was convinced that his name was engraved on the palms of God's hands, and—as God gripped me with love for this child—Zachary's name had now been imprinted on my heart. In fact, Zachary means "memory of the Lord." The seed of possibility that the Lord had planted in my heart years earlier, the "Zachary" who'd been held in my heart, had blossomed.

Through Zachary, God was teaching me how much he values *all* children. For years I'd poured my life into my own four kids: holding, feeding, wiping, rocking, laughing, crying, and comforting. And now God had gripped my heart with the conviction that every child has equal value in his eyes. I knew that Zachary's life was worth honoring. That his family wasn't able to care for him didn't negate Zachary's value in God's eyes or, now, in mine. Nothing could. And in ways I still couldn't fully grasp, the assurance in Psalm 68:6, that God sets the lonely in families, was unfolding before my eyes. God had chosen me to be Zachary's mom in death.

As quickly as I could, I made arrangements to sign the papers for his release. Just eighteen days after the coroner's call, the process was complete. In two and a half weeks I'd been set free to love and honor this baby boy.

ANGEL IN A BOW TIE

A dear friend, who'd buried her husband several years earlier, suggested I contact Indiana Funeral Care. Graciously, director David Ring was able to meet with me the day I finally had Zachary's paperwork in hand.

It was mid afternoon when I parked in the funeral home's near-empty lot. Carrying my purse and a file folder containing Zachary's paperwork, I made my way toward the building's heavy, white double doors. With each step I felt a sliver of the weight that parents who'd climbed the same stairs before me had borne.

Venturing inside, I was greeted warmly by David Ring, looking dapper in a blue bow tie and tortoiseshell-rimmed glasses. He introduced me to his staff and then directed me to a comfortable chair in a conference room to discuss arrangements.

When David's assistant popped in after about ten minutes, asking him to receive a phone call, I read a plaque titled "The Funeral" on the wall behind the chair where he'd been seated:

The funeral helps confirm the reality and finality of death.
Provides a climate for mourning and the expression of grief.
Allows the sorrows of one to become the sorrows of many.

As I reflected on those words and jotted them down to chew on later, I realized that at every turn of the journey unfolding before me I was learning so much. For years I had chased after God, eager to know him more. And yet, in what seemed to be the most horrendous circumstances for these forgotten children, I now felt closer to his heart than I ever had. Something had shifted inside me, releasing joy from a deep place I'd not known before. I mused that I never would have imagined that, on the heels of my mother's death and daughter's terrifying illness, I would be finding meaning, hope, and *life* in the place of sorrow and death. To a certain extent, I recognized the hope and peace I enjoyed as resonating deeply with the pattern of Jesus's life, death, and resurrection, but I still didn't fully understand it.

God was also teaching me that my idea of family was too small. For so many, including myself, "family" meant the people who raised me or the family I'd raised. Sometimes we stretch the boundaries enough to include folks like us from our churches. And yet, in ways I couldn't yet grasp, as I opened myself up to loving the poor and the homeless, the widow and the orphan—when I entered in to brokenness and pain and injustice—I found myself gathered up in God's lap as a member of a new kind of family.

His family.

When the director returned from his call, we discussed one of the most important decisions to be made that day: choosing baby Zachary's casket. Five months old when he died, he needed a casket sized for a baby, but larger than a newborn. We chose the date for the service and he explained that there wouldn't be time to custom order a new casket. Mr. Ring glanced over his inventory and told me that they had in stock the exact size that we needed. It was white satin with white trim. In that provision I saw, once again, how God had gone before me.

After finalizing all of the details, I thanked Mr. Ring and returned to my car. On the drive home, I mulled over Zachary's short life, trying to fit together the disparate pieces. I remembered my own babies at five months—the family and friends who doted over every giggle and gurgle. Had Zachary's mother gazed into his eyes as she fed him a bottle? Had his grandmother smiled upon him as he slept, imagining what his future might hold? Had his father made an effort to see him? Had anyone brought gifts to celebrate his birth? I had no way of knowing what it was like for him to live on the streets with a desperate mother. Yet I simply couldn't imagine a scenario in which a mother could release to a stranger the body of a child she'd borne.

When I arrived home I noticed a large brown box on my front porch. I was thankful the porch overhang protected the package from winter's elements. Picking up the box and carrying it inside, I anticipated the treasure I would find in the box. I set it down on the counter and carefully pulled off the shipping tape.

Peeling back a few layers of tissue paper, I pulled out a hand-stitched burial gown. A friend had recommended a Maine woman named Marcy, at Heaven Sent Baby, who generously created gorgeous gowns for abandoned babies. This one was made of pure white linen. Embroidered in pale blue, the prayerful seamstress had stitched, in perfect letters, "Zachary." Imagining it draped on his body, I wept. Carefully cradling the burial dress was the closest I would come to holding or seeing Zachary. The gown felt holy in my hands. The garment was a reminder that Zachary's *life* was holy. He had been created in God's image. His name in life and death was known to God.

I draped the gown across my arm and took it to my closet. Finding the smallest hanger I owned, I hung the white gown beside my own clothes.

ORPHANED IN DEATH

Before I delivered the gown to the funeral home the next day, I closed my eyes during my morning time with Jesus.

For years I'd been in the habit of starting my day this way. I'd learned through trial and error that each day I needed to talk with God, worship him, and listen for his voice by reading my Bible. As someone who's not a morning person, it doesn't come naturally! Each night before I go to bed, I set my alarm with enough time so I won't be rushed the next day.

That morning the Scripture to which the Lord directed me was James 1:27:

> Religion that God our Father accepts as pure and faultless is this: to look after orphans and widows in their distress and to keep oneself from being polluted by the world.

It was like I was encountering Scripture with new eyes and ears. Like so much of what God had been teaching me, I heard again the call for God's people to move into places of grief and sorrow. I was also seeing my world in fresh ways. I saw how those of us who had the ability to avoid suffering—through shopping, entertainment, vacation, and other comforts—distanced ourselves from death's sting. Fooling ourselves, I expect, we behaved as if death would always remain at a safe distance.

And God also continued to remind me that I had no idea what it was like to stand in the shoes of Zachary's mother. I no longer judged her for abandoning her child. And while I wrestled with God about how he could allow a child's life to end as Zachary's had, James's words reminded me that just as God had met Steve and me in the midst of our despair, God was passionately committed to caring for the poor and brokenhearted.

For three months I had imagined that the baby found in a dumpster would be my first funeral. Yet as the investigation into the identity of Baby Doe dragged on, Zachary found a home in my heart.

I delivered Zachary's gown to the funeral home three days before his funeral. After handing it to the administrative assistant, I returned to my car thinking about his small body that would soon be held, washed, and adorned. As I drove, my mind drifted to my mother's last months, when our relationship became as physical as it had been since I'd been dependent on her as a child. During our visits I fed, bathed, and dressed my mother just as she'd done for me and my six siblings. Just after my mother drew her last breath, I filled a porcelain cobalt blue bowl and washed her feet, my salty tears mingling with warm soapy water. As I neared home, I cried, grieving for the mother I'd loved my whole life and the infant I'd not had the privilege of knowing during his.

Zachary's service was held on an icy cold day in February of 2010. And though I'd already begun to prepare a worship service to honor the life of another baby whose name was not yet known, I now poured my heart and soul into creating a service that would honor Zachary with the dignity he too was due.

On the morning of February 12, I reached into the closet where Zachary's gown had so recently hung. Pulling on my black skirt and slipping into a pair of velvety heels, I imagined David Ring gently easing Zachary's body into his luxurious gown. Bundled up in my warmest coat, Steve and I drove to the funeral home so that we could follow the van carrying Zachary's casket to the cemetery.

When we arrived I saw a long parade of cars at the entrance. Those gathered included members of my family, church friends, my children's friends whose parents had taken them out of school to attend the service, as well as others who'd heard about Zachary's short life. These included cemetery staff, a few strangers, and a representative from a local crisis pregnancy center. Each one had shown up to remember a short life they believed was worth honoring. At the gates, Steve and I pulled ahead of them and they followed us, winding through the cemetery toward Zachary's site.

LULLABY FOR A BABY

Arriving at the plot, we parked and approached the burial area. A fresh snowfall made a beautiful white blanket to cover the ground and trees. The blue sky was pristine and the sunlight made the trees dance with the reflection of light. Steve gently carried the small casket to rest beside the open grave.

The service began with a welcome and a prayer. As my friend Jennifer sang Brahms's "Lullaby and Goodnight," many tears began to flow.

Looking out across the crowd, inviting them to join me in prayer, I announced that *we* were Zachary's spiritual family. As I began a prayer for him, standing beside his small casket, God reminded me of a vision he had given me many months before. In the vision, I was outside in the grass and stood in front of a small white casket. As this vision unfolded, I understood that God was letting me know that this "church" he was knitting together was one without walls. At the time I hadn't understood what the vision meant and had completely forgotten it. But God had not. As I stood in front of the tiny casket, heels sinking into the earth, looking out at the witnesses who had gathered to honor Zachary's life, I felt empowered by the vision God had so graciously given.

Before she died, my grandmother wore a bracelet with charms symbolizing her children and her children's children. Continuing the tradition, Steve began one for me after my first child, Lauren, was born. The four charms, engraved with birth dates and dangling from my wrist in birth order, represent Lauren, Andrew, Anna, and Caroline. A few days before the funeral, Steve added one more to my mother's bracelet: *Zachary*.

I glanced at some of the friends who stood with us at Zachary's graveside. Conversations with some over the previous week had reminded me how absurd our situation seemed to others. Some appeared baffled as I described my passion for Zachary. The disconnect reminded me that falling in love with a stranger's child, having never known that child in life, was difficult to comprehend. And yet I had connected at such a

visceral level to these vulnerable little ones. The months I'd spent waiting for the criminal investigation into Baby Doe's identity and death
had been laden with anticipation similar to what I experienced when I
was pregnant. And the essential part of me that God had knit into my
bones—to be a life-giver and a nurturer—had kicked into overdrive when
I learned of these children who'd been abandoned. So I recognized that
the drive fueling me to action was both natural, because it's how God
wired me, and supernatural, as God guided each new step.

As Steve rose to read Psalm 27 over the baby we'd grown to love, I
glanced down at Zachary's charm, dangling beside Caroline's. And as I
listened to the words waft over Zachary's body, the tenth verse suddenly
sounded different than I'd ever heard it before: "Though my father and
mother forsake me, the LORD will receive me."

Zachary *had* a mother. A father. Even a grandmother. And yet it was
the Lord who now—and always—received him with open arms.

The cry of the psalmist is the voice of one who longs to be home with
God. In it, I hear the voice of my Zachary:

> One thing I ask from the LORD,
>   this only do I seek:
> that I may dwell in the house of the LORD
>   all the days of my life,
> to gaze on the beauty of the LORD
>   and to seek him in his temple.
> For in the day of trouble
>   he will keep me safe in his dwelling;
> he will hide me in the shelter of his sacred tent
>   and set me high upon a rock. . . .
> Though my father and mother forsake me,
>   the LORD will receive me.
>   (Psalm 27:4–5, 10)

In the most profound way, the psalm announced Zachary's certain
homecoming. Although Zachary was, on earth, homeless and forsaken,
he would now and forever see the loving face of his Father. Wrapped in a

royal garment, he'd share a home with God and be held in his lap. He'd be fed by God's own hand and drink from a well of living water.

When Steve and I pulled away from Zachary's service that day, I rejoiced that baby Zachary's legacy would no longer be *homeless* or *abandoned*.

At last he had been *celebrated*.

As Steve drove us toward our safe, warm home, I wrestled to understand what God was up to. Was my assignment finished? Would I be allowed to bury the first baby who'd captured my heart? Humbled, I had no way of seeing what was unfolding before me. If I had depended on my own reasoning while watching the evening news three months earlier—about the sensibility of focusing on the needs of my own family, about the practicality of minding my own business, or even by saying a heartfelt prayer for the tragedy and forgetting it—I would have missed out on partnering with God in honoring Zachary's life. And now I didn't want my "reasoning" to get in the way of God's plan.

All I could do was say yes when God knocked again.

I was discovering it was all God needed.

Alfie's phone call had caught me completely off guard. I'd been willing to say yes to God about the baby who'd been found in a dumpster, but did God have even more in store for me? In ways I never would have imagined, God was opening my eyes to a world in need. And though I couldn't understand the heart or mind of Zachary's mother, God was assuring me that I didn't need to. I needed only to trust God and take the next step with him.

CHAPTER 3

Tim's Gift to Eli

Our interest in at-risk children didn't begin out of the blue. Two years earlier, Steve and I had said another yes that was continuing to transform our lives in beautiful ways. We champion an organization called Safe Families for Children, a national movement of compassion offering safe, loving homes where parents can voluntarily have their children cared for while parents restore stability in their own lives. Safe Families introduced us to Eli, who lived with us for twelve weeks. As his mom became better-resourced, he was able to return home to live with her. Keeping families intact is the beautiful vision of Safe Families. Eli melted our hearts the moment we laid eyes on him, and though he now lives with his mom, he still visits us regularly.

The summer after we buried Zachary, four-year-old Eli stayed with us for a few days. School was out and Caroline's high school friends were gathered around the pool behind our house chattering and giggling like only teen girls can.

Eli scooped water out of the pool in plastic cups and poured it on the girls' legs as they laid out in the sun. I peeked up from my journal every now and then to make sure he wasn't bugging them. Having not yet learned to swim, Eli understood that to be in the water he needed to be wearing his life vest.

His curiosity, however, fueled his overconfidence. Eli stepped into the shallow end of the pool and, unexpectedly buoyed by the water, immediately lost his footing and began to sink. I saw him struggling right away. Dropping my journal, I jumped into the water and yanked him up from under it. As he gasped to regain his breath, we looked at each other, mirroring one another's fear. As I held him even tighter, he started crying and quickly apologized.

The fright reminded me how quickly tragedy can strike. After we strapped Eli into his life vest and he was happily kicking his feet on the side of the pool, I continued to nurse what-ifs. What if I had dashed inside for a moment and the girls hadn't noticed him? What if Eli's designated "safe" family wasn't safe *enough*? What would it be like for his mother to have not even had the *chance* to protect her son?

Catching myself and my runaway thoughts, I decided I wasn't willing to let them get the best of me. A few years before, I'd picked up a book called *Pray with Purpose, Live with Passion*, by Debbie Williams.[2] This book changed my spiritual life, as much as any book ever has, by waking me up to claim the mighty character of God. In its pages I discovered a method of prayer that I've continued to use daily, praying through the ABCs of God's character: "Abba, Advocate, Almighty, Anointed One, Beloved Son, Bread, Breath, Comforter . . ." Unable to return to my journaling, and still rattled by Eli's sudden plunge, I began silently praying to the Father that Eli and I shared. That we could have lost him so easily terrified me, and I called on God to be Eli's Guardian, Helper, and Protector.

Eli recovered from the scare quicker than I did. As I kept glancing toward him, watching him kicking his strong legs in the pool, my mind wandered to Baby Doe, still on my heart after all these months. How had that child died? Had it been an accident that happened in the blink of an eye, the way Eli had just slipped into the pool? Could the kind of help Safe Families provided for Eli have saved that child's life?

I still had no way of knowing.

A MOM IN NEED

Throughout that summer I continued to call Alfie every Friday to inquire about my very first Baby Doe. I'd called when Eli was visiting. I'd even called during a trip to Michigan. Detectives had still not identified the body or located the baby's mother.

In mid August though, when I made my weekly phone call to Alfie, she ventured, "I have this mom who needs a headstone." Her voice sounded hesitant.

"Do you buy headstones for people?" she queried. "I didn't know if I should ask you for this . . . "

Do I buy headstones for people?

Honestly, I didn't know. I knew that God had called me to stay engaged with the baby who'd been found in a dumpster. And when Alfie hesitantly asked, six months earlier, whether I might consider burying Zachary, I had felt God's nudge to do it. Burying him with the kind of dignified service my mom had received seemed like exactly the right thing to do. Of course I bought him a headstone.

Still, I didn't yet know whether buying headstones for people was something I *did*.

This wasn't a baby, Alfie explained. A thirteen-year-old boy named Tim Bray had, along with his friends, snuck into a city pool on the night of June 22. It was a Tuesday. As teenage boys are wont to do, they had been goofing off. Though the details were murky, whether he'd fallen into the water accidentally or been pushed by a friend, Tim Bray lost his balance and lost his life. He'd been his mother's only child.

A chill shot through my body as I remembered Eli's brush with danger beside my pool.

This was a different direction than God had recently called me. Tim was clearly older than either Zachary or the baby I continued to hold in my heart, but there was something else that was different as well. Now there was a mother whom I could know and connect with.

"This mom is really grieving," Alfie continued.

I weighed Alfie's request in my heart. It felt so much like every other step of this unlikely journey. Because of Alfie, a door was opening. Through it I saw an adolescent son, a desperate grieving mom. Was this a door I was being called to walk through? Though nothing in my spirit seemed to prohibit the possibility, I proceeded cautiously.

"Alfie," I answered, "I'd love to meet that mom. Would that be possible?"

Alfie said she'd like to try to arrange it.

I was anxious to meet Tim Bray's mother, and I was also itchy to meet one other person: Alfie herself.

A SURPRISING CORONER

Alfie's office, a small freestanding building that's dwarfed by the monster Lucas Oil Stadium across the street, is in a run-down part of town. The glass door on the outside of Alfie's office reads *Forensic Science*. I expected the morgue to be cool, sanitized, impersonal. Pulling open the tall, heavy door, the morgue appeared much as I had imagined, though I never dreamed of the warm reception waiting inside.

The staff was unexpectedly delightful. I identified myself to the friendly secretary. After she buzzed Alfie, I waited for a woman to appear in a sterile white lab coat.

When Alfie came out front to meet me, I was immediately taken with her. She was short, with beautiful brown skin, and her broad, joyful smile hinted at what I'd soon discover to be her larger-than-life personality. She had a deep side part, with sweeping blond bangs across her forehead. That day she was wearing big red glasses. In fact, everything about her was colorful: a bright flowery blouse, bold earrings and necklace, and even bright, jazzy heels. She exuded confidence and charisma.

Alfie was not the "coroner" I'd been expecting.

For that matter, no one who worked in her office was what I expected. Rather than some dismal, depressed drones, during my visit I found a tight-knit group of folks who cared about one another and cared about the families they served. Though many began working at the city coroner's office intending to stay for a year or two, many of them stayed. And stayed.

You know how, in television crime shows, the crime scene cordoned off with yellow tape is quickly swarming with cops and detectives and other people in official uniforms? One of those people is the coroner. The coroner's job can't be neatly fit into a nine-to-five schedule—or any schedule. These servants are on call twenty-four hours a day, listening to police radios. These are the ones who must knock on a family's door and deliver the most difficult news.

"Your son fell into a pool and drowned."

"Your husband was killed in an auto accident as he was driving home from work."

"We found your sister's body."

Throughout the course of a criminal investigation, distraught family members will call the coroner's office for updates. Until the body is released to a licensed funeral home, the coroner is in contact with that family.

A coroner can look at a crime scene, and it may look different to her than it does to everyone else. Family members may look at a death and view it as accidental, insisting there were no drugs involved; it wasn't the ex-boyfriend; there was no abuse. But the coroner's eye has been trained to see what others do not.

It's not a position I envy.

Based on what I saw in Alfie's office, her staff was doing a difficult job with kindness and compassion.

THE QUESTION I'D BEEN WANTING TO ASK

I had asked to meet Alfie thirty minutes before Tim's mother was scheduled to arrive because there was one question I'd been wanting to ask her. Over the months, as I kept calling about the baby found in a dumpster, I'd expected Alfie to tire of me quickly. I knew she was a busy woman, but she always seemed to have time for my call. That intrigued me. Then, she'd called me to ask if my "organization" would consider burying baby Zachary. She didn't have to do that. And now, this. She had completed her work on Tim's body several months earlier, but she was still engaged, caring for a hurting family.

Alfie greeted me and led me to an intimate conference room.

At last sitting face-to-face, I looked into Alfie's eyes and asked, "Why do you care?"

Her face revealed that my query wasn't what she'd been expecting.

Mulling it over for a moment, she replied, "Well . . . I was raised to care about people and be compassionate."

She explained that her dad had been a policeman. Her husband was too. She'd learned from their experience that either you could become callous or you could really care for people.

"I was also raised going to church," she added.

"Yes," I pushed, "but who is Jesus to you?"

That's what I most wondered.

Without hesitating, Alfie answered, "He is my everything."

In that moment, we became sisters. We shared about our faith. We learned about each other's families. Our relationship shifted from business to personal. We even prayed together.

Before we lifted our heads from prayer, there was a knock at the door.

Cracking the door open about a foot, Alfie's assistant announced, "The family is here."

FAMILY

Family?

I'd been expecting to meet only Tim's mom. Perhaps she'd brought a sister or mother with her for support. I already felt nervous, and somehow having another person to meet made me even more so.

"How many?" Alfie asked, unfazed.

"Oh," the assistant guessed, "about twelve, I'd say."

"Well," Alfie reasoned, "this conference room is not going to work. Why don't you show them into the big conference room."

Alfie's assistant left to help the family find the big conference room.

My heart raced. Twelve? What had I gotten myself into? I let Alfie know I was anxious and she reassured me that it would be fine. It wasn't clear to me yet whether Alfie realized I wasn't actually leading an organization. It was more like I was stumbling into one.

Inhaling a big breath of Alfie's unflagging confidence, we stepped outside the small conference room and she led me toward this family. Outside in the foyer we climbed a spiral staircase toward the large conference room. With every step we ascended, I prayed. "God, I have no idea what is going to be on the other side of that door! I don't know what shape this mom or family is in. Help!"

Over the next few years it became a plea I prayed often—one God never failed to answer.

Alfie opened the door and ushered me in.

The room was filled with family members, representing what appeared to be three generations. There were teens who hovered around

Tim's age. There were a few little one-, three-, and four-year-olds. There were aunties, cousins, and a grandmother.

Alfie introduced me to Tim's mother.

"Addy, this is Linda," she said. "And Linda, this is Addy."

Addy was six months pregnant and very emotional. Rocking back and forth, she rubbed her stomach.

We shook hands, and I looked for a seat. The only chair left at the conference table was at the head. I sat down, resting my Bible and journal on the table. As I glanced around the room, it occurred to me that no one in the family knew exactly why I was there. *I* didn't know exactly why I was there! All any of us knew is that Alfie had let them know I'd like to help.

None of us knew how our time together would unfold.

"Okay," I began, "tell me about Tim."

It was all I needed to do.

For an hour, Tim's mom, his cousins, his grandmother, his aunts and uncles, and even one of his friends described the young man they'd lost.

But there was one discrepancy: the character they described sounded nothing like the one presented in the media. Though I'd been away in Michigan when Tim had died, I'd gone online to check out the story. The young man described in these news reports came across as a delinquent with a negligent mom, out after curfew with his friends, breaking into a city swimming facility.

Tim's family described a young man who volunteered with a dynamic neighborhood organization called Rebuilding the Wall. RTW makes home ownership affordable to low-income families by drawing from the talent in the community to rehabilitate vacant and abandoned homes. Tim was active in a Bible study the organization ran, as well. He had been a bright kid who did well in school. And for the second year in a row he'd won a scholarship to attend summer camp. Tim was scheduled to leave for camp four days after he died.

He sounded a lot like one of my kids. He'd been riding his bike with his friends at nine at night on the longest day of the year. It was still *light* outside. He and his buddies had jumped a fence. But Tim didn't grow up in the neighborhood where my kids grew up. He didn't have a pool in his back yard, like mine had. He'd never had a swim lesson. He didn't look like my kids. Though I could only speculate, I believed that if one of my kids had been in the same position as Tim, it would have been spun in the media as "tragic" rather than "criminal."

As others shared about Tim, Addy paced the room. Visibly agitated, talking nonstop, she kept repeating, "They didn't like him because he had cornrows in his hair that day." Apparently she'd seen the same news reports I had.

After I'd learned more about who Tim was, I explained to the family a bit about the ministry God seemed to be birthing. I shared the gospel with them, read Scripture, and prayed.

In that conference room I was discovering that what God was calling me to was more expansive than only giving babies honor in death. Learning about who Tim actually had been—in such stark contrast to the way society had portrayed him—revealed something new. Tim's family would honor him in death with a moving memorial ceremony, but God was showing me, through Tim's story, that establishing a legacy of dignity would be equally important. How Tim would be remembered, by his family and by his community, mattered. Part of that legacy would be his headstone, and I began to wonder if there would be even more.

As we wrapped up, I explained, "It would be my joy to buy Tim a headstone."

What happened next was like nothing I had ever experienced in my life.

A FAMILY'S HEARTACHE

As if in a single voice, Tim's family began wailing together, overcome with gratitude. Honestly, it was almost more than I could endure. As was often the case, it would have been much easier to send a check than to sit in that conference room and bear, alongside them, the weight of their overwhelming grief. Instead, I sat still as I experienced an emotional tidal wave.

When I'd buried my mother the previous year, it had not once occurred to me to be grateful for a headstone.

The expectations of Tim's family were so different from my own.

And the gift of a headstone was a palpable expression of the disparities between us. Addy and her relatives couldn't believe that he was going to get a headstone. Tim had been buried in what the community considered a pauper's cemetery. It wasn't landscaped or well cared for. Tim had friends and uncles buried there, but none had headstones. Family members identified these cemetery residents as a drug dealer, a gang member, a victim of a drive-by shooting.

That wasn't Tim.

Addy knew it, her family knew it, and now I knew it. In fact, I could see that it made Addy visibly uncomfortable that he'd been laid to rest beside them, because of the ways they'd died.

"My Tim," Addy insisted, still fretful, "was a good kid."

I was already convinced.

As I left the building and walked to my car, I was struck by how the grief of Addy and her family looked so different from grief within my own community. A lot of those in my circles—privileged, educated, white—had struggled to allow me to grieve well. As I processed the loss of my mother, and also as Steve and I accompanied our daughter through her excruciating illness, many friends in our social circles wanted to hear me say that I was doing well. They understood the importance of healthy grieving, but they wanted to know I was working through my grief personally. Privately. Quietly. This is one of the reasons Addy's family was such a gift to me. To spend time among those who lamented so openly was a precious gift from God to me on this journey. Addy's authentic expression of grief, without any need to mask painful emotions, gave me the permission I needed to be authentic before God and before others. A woman I never expected to meet led me into the way of healing.

GOOD KID WITH A GOOD MOM

It took two months for Tim's headstone to be completed.

By the time we all met again at the cemetery, to dedicate the granite headstone, Addy was eight months pregnant. Steve and Caroline were there too. It felt like a sacred gift to be with Addy and with Tim's extended family again. When I hugged Addy good-bye that day, I had a sense that our relationship was just beginning.

I called Addy occasionally to see how she was feeling, and our friendship continued to blossom. Addy confided in me that although she read her Bible, she didn't always understand it. When she most recently suspected she was pregnant, Addy had visited a local crisis pregnancy center where she had heard the gospel and was given a Bible. It rested on her nightstand, unopened, until Tim died. When she had nowhere else to turn, she'd opened it, looking for answers.

A few weeks after the headstone dedication, the Lord woke me up in the middle of the night with thoughts of Addy. I had this sudden idea that I needed to disciple her and invite her into a Bible study. Some friends of mine had done a study they raved about called Operation Timothy.[3]

Really, God?

I called her in the morning to test the waters. The moment I asked her, Addy agreed.

A few days later we met at a coffee shop to begin our Bible study. Because Eli was staying with Steve and me that week, he came along too. Addy loved cuddling with him and helping him choose crayons for his coloring book. Every so often, his little hand would reach up and grab her muffin or sip her drink. As I watched her gently nurture Eli, it was easy to imagine the kind of mom she'd been to Tim.

Addy and I met just that one time before Addy gave birth. Her son, Julian, was born on December 23. She called Steve and me from the hospital to share the good news, and we were the first visitors to arrive.

"The Lord told me this morning that you were going to be the first ones here, even before my mom," she gushed as we entered the room, adding, "I knew you would come. I am so glad you didn't bring Caroline."

That surprised us because Addy *loved* our youngest, who was just Tim's age. Caroline had been around a lot and had walked through the early days of the ministry with us. She was at every event, including Tim's headstone dedication. Though I'd missed the memorial for Tim due to travel, Caroline and Steve had attended together.

The moment we stepped into her room, I washed my hands and scooped Julian up out of Addy's arms, and was gently rocking him back and forth. Addy's broad smile dimmed just long enough to ask us a serious question.

"I didn't want to ask in front of Caroline," she began, "but can Caroline be Julian's godmother?"

Steve and I looked at each other with surprise and delight.

"Go ahead and ask her," we suggested. "She will *love* it."

And that's how my Caroline became Julian's godmother. Though some find it surprising, I see it as an outward sign of the way God has knit our families' hearts together in love. In one of my favorite books on suffering, *A Grace Disguised*, Jerry Sittser writes, "But loss does not have to isolate us or make us feel lonely. Though it is a solitary experience we must face alone, loss is also a common experience that can lead us to community. It can create a community of brokenness. We must enter the darkness of loss alone, but once there we will find others with whom we can share life together."[4]

In ways I wasn't yet fully able to grasp, those unexpected others who now shared my life were being used by God to heal my own heart.

REDEMPTION IN THE WATER

Addy, consummately proud of her son, wanted Tim to be remembered the way he really was. And I wanted to partner with her to do it. Addy's passion confirmed the inkling I'd received from the Spirit the day Addy and I had first met, about establishing a lasting legacy of dignity.

The Center for Disease Control and Prevention reports that for people under twenty-nine years of age, drowning is one of the top three causes of unintentional injury death.[5] Black children who are eleven and twelve years old drown in swimming pools at ten times the rates of white children of the same age! Statistics also prove that one of the most effective drowning prevention strategies is to teach basic swimming skills.

Addy and I decided together that teaching urban kids water safety and swim skills would be a wonderful way to honor Tim's memory. We met with the mayor's office to discuss partnering with Indy Parks to establish a scholarship program in Tim's name. On the first anniversary of his death we held a big event at Douglass Park, where Tim had drowned, to announce the program. Caroline carried six-month-old Julian while Addy and I served as organizers.

In addition to educating the public on startling drowning statistics, guest speakers also highlighted the importance of the park system, celebrating its community atmosphere and the way it provided a safe place for children who lived in the urban environment. Addy even noted that Tim had called the park his "back yard."

During one of the guest's speeches I peeked over the crowd and saw Alfie, dressed in a bright turquoise dress and summer sandals. If it hadn't been for Alfie, we might not have all been gathered. I silently prayed that she'd not have to examine the body of one more Indianapolis child lost to drowning. I know that was Addy's hope and prayer as well.

Today Tim is not remembered at Douglass Park as the bad kid who drowned; he's the one whose smiling face beams on the bronze wall plaque at the front gate of the pool. He's also the one supplying a week's worth of swim lessons to kids at Douglass Park every single summer. Today children run up to Addy while she's out running errands, and say, "Miss Addy, I took lessons from Tim!" Addy is now the mother of a legacy. She is the mother who is protecting her son's memory. To see her healing through Tim's legacy is incredible.

Last summer, four years after he lost his footing and slipped underwater in my backyard pool, one of those children who received the swim lessons he needed, in Tim's name, was my precious eight-year-old Eli.

Addy could not have been more delighted.

I had seen what God did when I said my small yes to calling the coroner's office. I had even seen how God blessed the worship service that honored Zachary's short life. But now God called me to stand face-to-face with a brokenhearted mother and her family in their darkest hour. A voice in my head nagged, insistent that I hadn't been trained in pastoral care or grief counseling. I wasn't sure I had what it took. And yet, despite the fact that I felt entirely ill-equipped, I discovered that God had not only prepared me to care for Tim's grieving family but was also healing my own heart. By allowing me to witness precious Addy's authentic and transforming grief—before others and before God—God was setting me free.

CHAPTER 4

The Wait Was Over

I continued to phone Alfie at the coroner's office every Friday throughout the spring and summer and into the fall. While clearing the morning's breakfast dishes off our blue-tiled countertop, over a year after a baby's body had been found in a city dumpster, I dialed once again. Honestly, I expected little. But today Alfie informed me that the baby and the baby's mother had been identified.

I stopped shuffling dishes the moment I realized that this conversation would be different from the fifty or so that had preceded it. It was what I'd been waiting for.

It wasn't until that moment that I realized my hope had worn thin. Though I knew that there would eventually be a service for this child, I'd long ago stopped expecting the police to find the baby's mother. And if they ever did, would she be the way she'd been painted in the news? Would she be a cruel monster? A desperate addict? A deranged woman who didn't know what she'd done? Were other children in her home at risk? The ugliest stereotypes of mothers living in poverty, facing untold adversities, flooded my mind. I didn't even consider, at the time, that the mother might be someone very much like me.

AN UNEXPECTED VISIT

Before my mind drifted further, Alfie explained that, earlier in the week, homicide detectives had knocked on the door of a woman named Nichole Moody. The forty-one-year-old had given birth in 2008, but her son had not lived. When the detectives told her they believed they'd found his remains, she protested, saying that her child had been cremated. Alfie had learned, though, that other evidence in the dumpster suggested that the funeral home that had taken possession of her son was somehow responsible for the illegal disposal. It's what led the detective to Moody's door. They asked her to visit the coroner's office to identify what they believed to be the remains of her child.

When Moody met with Alfie, to do what every parent prays she'll never have to do, she recognized and identified her son's gorgeous, soft, wavy hair. The pattern matched the hospital photo that she cherished. After Nichole identified her son's body at the morgue, Alfie gently explained to her that there was someone else who was interested in her son's case and might like to meet her.

As I sat down on a stool beside my kitchen counter to take it all in, Alfie offered me the opportunity to meet Nichole the following day. It was what I'd been so eager to do for over a year. As we continued to talk, Alfie shared just enough about the case to convince me that Nichole Moody was not the heartless mother the media had portrayed. Instead, she was a mother who desperately longed to hold her son the way I delighted in cradling my son Andrew as an infant. She was a mother who had been wronged in a cruel way.

AN UNLIKELY MEETING

The following morning I was waiting in the lobby of the coroner's office when Nichole arrived. She was clearly agitated. Wearing jeans and a burgundy jacket, the wild-eyed woman stormed in chugging an energy drink. Gray streaks peppered her tight ponytail. Still grieving the loss of her firstborn child, and now traumatized once again after identifying his remains, she'd come to meet the curious stranger who was interested in being involved in her life.

Delicately, with compassion, Alfie introduced us.

As our gazes met, each of us sized up the other.

I imagined what Nichole saw when she looked at me: tall, blond, thin, white, middle-aged, rich.

When I looked at Nichole, I saw, in some ways, a stereotype as well. She was, to my eye, a poor black woman who'd not had many breaks in her life. But more than that, I saw someone who was suffering. She never stopped moving, pacing back and forth as if trapped and looking for an escape.

"Hi," I offered, extending my hand. "I'm Linda."

Nichole looked me over as if she was deciding whether or not to return the courtesy.

"Hi," she grunted, still deciding what she thought of me. Hesitant, distracted, she shook my hand.

Our conversation was brief, yet in our short exchange Nichole told me that her son's name was Nicholas.

After months of wondering, I relished the sound of it: Nicholas. During the season I'd been waiting for this child's release, I wondered if he'd been given a name. I'd also become more convinced than ever that every child deserves a name and is worthy of being known, loved, and honored. For months on end, as I poured over my Bible to make sense of what seemed so senseless, the irrefutable value of every person sung from each page. In the Lord's promise to a suffering people through Isaiah, I heard the promise that was for Nicholas as well: "I will give them an everlasting name that will endure forever" (Isaiah 56:5).

Nicholas finally had his name back.

I did my best to explain to Nichole the odd series of events by which I'd come to so love her son. And as the words fell from my lips, I suddenly knew, in my deep places, that I now had a new purpose. This was no longer just about the precious bones waiting for burial. I knew, as I stood before her, that my new purpose was to honor this distraught mother by offering her a burial that honored her son. I didn't want her to have to endure the costs and burden of organizing, planning, and making decisions. This was a gift I wanted to give to Nichole.

If she was to accept, I suddenly realized, she would have to sign over her son's body to another funeral home. How on earth could I ask that of a woman who'd been unspeakably violated by those in whose care her baby had first been entrusted? Realizing that Nichole might be rattled by the necessary legality, I wanted to ease her burden.

Looking Nichole in the eye, touching her arm, I gently explained, "I loved your child and I love you. I have wanted to give this baby a proper burial, and it's still something I'd like to do for you. It's a gift I'd like to give you. Do you think you can trust me?"

Nichole Moody suddenly became calm.

Knowing the weight of what I was asking, I quickly interjected, "Don't answer. Sleep on it and pray about it. Decide if you can trust me, and I'll call you tomorrow."

Then, after our short time together, we parted.

I crossed the street to a city parking garage where I fell into my pearl blue Mercedes. Nichole walked to the bus stop where a bus would take her home. I knew we were both thinking of the other, and we were both thinking of Nicholas. Any passerby who'd noticed us together might have made some of the same assumptions I did about which one of us was most likely to be on the giving and receiving ends of gift giving. And while that passing stranger wouldn't have been entirely wrong, they could not have imagined the relationship and gifts that would continue to be shared between us and, in time, through us to others. Every person has something to give.

When I phoned Nichole the following day, I repeated the one question that mattered: "Will you trust me?"

After several seconds, the answer on the other end of the line was the one I'd prayed for.

"Yes."

ONE BRAVE MOTHER

Two days later, Nichole hopped back on the bus to return downtown to sign a legal document authorizing the release of her son's body to Indiana Funeral Care.

The courage that required, after all that had happened the first time Nicholas's body was entrusted to a funeral home, was seismic. Because Indiana Funeral Care had been wonderful to work with on Zachary's service, I knew they'd treat Nichole well, but in the moment she carefully penned her signature in Alfie's office, she had no way of knowing that. She also had no way of knowing that the odd blond stranger who'd fallen in love with her son also cared for her.

After signing the document with Alfie, Nichole and I met at the Social Services office, where she was hoping to get assistance with her utility bill, to discuss the burial. Appearing as she had the first time we'd met at Alfie's office, Nichole was dressed in worn jeans and an oversized sweatshirt, her hair pulled back into a rubber band.

As we sat side by side in the waiting room, Nichole babbled disjointed thoughts about her unsuccessful attempts to contact the funeral home to receive her son's remains. She listed excuses she'd heard from the office manager. The many unreturned calls. She spewed the string of disjointed thoughts as if *she* was now on trial, as if I believed her to be the unidentified "bad mother" in the news reports. Yet what I heard was that she'd done all she could with limited emotional resources during that dark season. She didn't yet realize that God's great compassion for her had rooted and sprouted in my heart. Any judgment I'd felt for the unknown mother had evaporated.

Nichole was very agitated and loud, as if no one else were in the room. She continued to rant about the corrupt funeral home that had so disrespected Nicholas's body and she rambled on about wanting her brother, sister, and mother to attend the service, and kept repeating that she needed to get her hair done. She asked if I was the police.

As we waited to be called, I lowered my voice in hopes she might do the same. Nichole had begun to share very precious, private details of her story and I felt very protective, wanting to guard it from nearby listening ears. She had lived a rough life. When Nichole got pregnant at seventeen, her mother made her have an abortion—her story wound through several more difficult decades until this most recent painful chapter.

After Nicholas had died, Nichole was distraught. She was emotionally devastated that the child for whom she'd longed, the only child she'd ever birthed, had died after living only thirteen hours. Nichole had remained in the hospital for weeks. Since then she'd suffered from depression and substance abuse. Continuing to deal with health complications, including the dangerous remaining presence of placenta tissue that should have been passed after birth, her health crisis was still unresolved. Nichole shared that now, more than two years after Nicholas's delivery, her doctor wanted to perform laser surgery to remove tissue still clinging to her uterus. Over time, he'd warned, it could become life-threatening. I couldn't fathom the depth of Nichole's agony: grieving a child while struggling to recover from such harrowing post-delivery complications.

My mind flashed back fifteen years to the birth of my daughter Caroline, born via emergency cesarean section because I was hemorrhaging due to placenta previa. As the doctors worked frantically to control my bleeding, Steve feared he'd lose both his wife and his new daughter.

While still recovering after Caroline's birth, I was invited by some older women at church into a Bible study to dive deep into God's Word. When I agreed, I couldn't have imagined the way these women would continue to dig deep into my life. Over the last two decades, those women have walked with me through my darkest days: heartaches with children, difficult seasons in marriage, Anna's brush with death, losing my mother and then my father. Bravely walking with me through those seasons of loss wasn't requisite. Many folks, even well-meaning ones, protect themselves by withdrawing during seasons of crisis. Though these women could have chosen to avoid my suffering, they bravely entered into every aspect of my life—listening, comforting, fasting, and praying.

As I listened to Nichole's story, I was keenly aware how different our experiences of suffering had been. Though the doctor was warning her that her condition was still life-threatening, Nichole didn't care. She hated hospitals and announced, with an angry snarl, that she didn't care if it killed her.

Nichole's physical and emotional pain seemed to seep from every pore. In moments of her rant, she announced that she was a mean person. And that no one could make her go to church. I understood, in those moments, why it had been so hard for her to return to the first funeral home to seek Nicholas's ashes. His body represented all she'd been trying to forget. But any woman who's been pregnant or delivered a baby knows that a mother does *not* forget.

"I feel like Nicholas has been following me the last two years," she grieved.

In her vulnerability I heard that Nichole was in desperate need of closure.

"What do you want for your baby now?" I asked gently.

Nichole reported that she'd paid $75 for Nicholas to be cremated, the cheapest option available. But as we spoke, she softened to reveal that she would really have preferred to choose a proper casket, funeral, burial.

As we sat side by side in the molded plastic chairs lining the waiting room of Social Services, Nichole also continued to circle around the circumstances of her abortion. Having walked with other women who'd endured abortions, I knew that it could be as important to grieve the loss of a child to abortion as it was to grieve the one lost to miscarriage, stillbirth, or other infant loss. After the third time she spoke of it, I got an idea.

"Nichole, when we bury Nicholas, would you like to remember and memorialize the first baby you lost as well?"

"Yes," she affirmed, "I would."

I saw a visible calm fall over her.

Hesitant to go too deep too fast, I ventured, "One of the things that can be really helpful is to name the child who was lost. Would you like to choose a name for the baby who was aborted?"

I hoped my query wouldn't upset her further.

Without hesitation, she replied, "Her name is Natasha."

For more than two decades Nichole had held this baby in her heart, missing her. Natasha would have been twenty-three. Nichole's maternal instinct told her that her child had been a girl and she'd chosen to name her Natasha. In my informal ministry among women I knew that when children could be named, they could also be grieved. Some even choose to name and mourn their babies decades after they've been lost. Nichole was on the right track.

When a social worker called Nichole's name, I stood to leave.

"Can I give you a hug?" I asked.

Pausing to consider my request, she offered a dull, "No."

Respecting Nichole's boundaries, I said good-bye and left the office. As I walked back to my car, my heart and mind were filled with thoughts of Nichole's lost daughter.

Certain that the book of life held Natasha's name, I ordered a special charm for Nichole later that day that said *Natasha*. I also ordered another charm necklace with both of her children's names engraved on it. It reads, "Trust the Lord, Proverbs 3:5." When we met to discuss the funeral service the following week, I gave Nichole the necklace and Natasha's loose charm as a tangible sign that, in addition to Nicholas, Natasha had existed. Natasha had not been forgotten. She'd not been lost. She'd not been unwanted by her heavenly Father.

And I didn't think Natasha had been unwanted by her mother either.

HONORING NICHOLAS

On the morning of the service planned for Nicholas, in October 2010, Steve and I drove to Indiana Funeral Care where we followed the hearse carrying Nicholas's body. Nichole had decided that our honoring of Natasha that day, in our hearts, would be kept private between us and the funeral director. When we arrived at the cemetery Nichole's family was waiting in cars at the gate. Those vehicles fell in line and we proceeded to the site where Nicholas A. Lamonte Moody would be buried. I learned later that, since Nichole and I had met, her mother had not believed that a service would really happen. She'd told Nichole that she thought I wouldn't show up. While I understood that she had no reason to trust me, I knew it must have made the waiting even more difficult for Nichole.

When we slowed to a stop, Nichole emerged from her mother's car and she looked beautiful. When I'd given Nichole her charms, she'd told me that she wanted to wear a hat to her baby's funeral, and I found her a black hat with a round turned-up brim and flowery embellishment on top. Her hair was ironed out straight and worn long. She wore a dark gray suit with heels. The necklace with her children's names hung around her neck. Had I not known her, I would not have recognized her as the distraught woman I met two weeks earlier.

I had waited thirteen months to speak blessings over this mother, her children, and all who would attend. Steve, Anna, and Caroline attended the service. I took Caroline out of school and several of her friends' moms did the same. Nichole's extended family was there. And I was so pleased to catch a glimpse of Tim Bray's mom, Addy, wearing black slacks and a long black coat. Just as the service was beginning, she slipped in quietly, eyes down.

The only snag of the day was that the gown I'd ordered from Maine for Nicholas hadn't arrived on time. After scrambling around town I had found one with a cross applique stitched onto the chest of a white linen gown that had a thin piece of fine blue satin ribbon woven through the hemline and tied in a bow. Knowing I'd wanted an embroidered gown for Nicholas, Steve located a local seamstress who could help. Steve drove out to her home late at night and waited for her to stitch "Nicholas" in blue at the neckline. When she heard what the gown was for, she hadn't charged us for her work.

Steve now opened the service with prayer and then I read Scripture. The verse the Lord gave me to honor baby Nicholas was Isaiah 49:16. "See, I have engraved you on the palms of my hands."

I had prayed for days about whom to ask to sing at the service. Though at the time I only knew of Christopher Wilburn through mutual friends, when I saw him at the church we both attend, the Lord clearly said, "He's the one." Chris, an accomplished opera singer and an African-American like Nicholas, was an officer with the Indianapolis Metropolitan Police Department. I knew that Nichole—and others in crisis who depend on investigative officers for details and closure—were suspicious of police officers, and of coroners, for failing to identify Nicholas's body sooner. I was delighted when Officer Wilburn accepted my invitation to sing. And that he was blessing Nichole in such a palpable way felt like one of many redemptive elements of the day. One song he chose to sing, bringing tears to every eye, was a poignant presentation of "Lullaby and Goodnight."

I shared a brief message based on the Old Testament story of Joseph. Joseph, the eleventh son of his father, the patriarch Jacob, was the first son of Rachel. Jacob made no bones that Joseph, born of his favorite wife, was his favorite son. At the violent hands of his older brothers, Joseph was abducted and sold into slavery. Jacob, tricked into believing his son had been killed, was deceived—as Nichole had been!—as to where his son was. Joseph had been thrown away, as Nicholas had been, and was finally reunited with the parent who'd never stopped longing for him. Nicholas's body had been returned to Nichole and his spirit was held, eternally, in his heavenly Father's arms.

At the conclusion of the service, we released a few dozen balloons, each with a Scripture tied to the string, gently waving in the breeze. As I watched them float to the heavens, I felt the calming presence of the Holy Spirit.

After the service, the funeral director opened the casket just a crack so that Nichole could slip the loose charm honoring Natasha into Nicholas's casket.

As mourners shared their condolences with Nichole, I spotted Tim Bray's mother, Addy. I knew she'd never met Nichole. The week prior, Addy had been very clear in letting me know that she would be attending Nicholas's service not for me, but for Nichole. It was the eighth child's funeral she'd taken it upon herself to attend since burying Tim four months earlier. Laying aside her own grief, Addy kept showing up to funerals of children she'd never met to support other grieving mothers. I saw Addy begin to shine as she slowly returned to life, bravely entering into the suffering of others, and I was reminded how slivers of light can illuminate the darkest days.

In his book on grief, Jerry Sittser offers, "Loss can also make us more. In the darkness we can still find the light. In death we also find life."[6] Had Addy chosen to harden her heart, walling herself off from the hurt of others, darkness and death's sting would have won. But in her brave movement into the suffering of others, I witnessed Addy being vivified. As God continued to heal each of our hearts, Addy and I were walking very similar paths.

After the service Addy, whose own charm for Tim was worn bundled under her black wool coat, approached Nichole. With kindness and concern, she handed Nichole a card. The front of the envelope was blank.

"Sorry, I didn't know your name," she began. "I lost my child too. Also a boy. We have a lot in common."

I simply stood back, silent, and watched Addy minister the love and comfort of Jesus to a mother with whom she so deeply connected.

It was the women's first meeting, but it wouldn't be their last.

NOURISHED AT THE HOLIDAYS

A few weeks after Nicholas's service, I was able to connect with Nichole on the Monday before Thanksgiving. She sounded delighted to hear from me and told me that one of the balloons we'd released at the funeral had ended up in her boss's yard! We chatted about what we'd each be doing for the holiday and what we'd be eating.

"Do you make dressing?" Nichole asked.

"Oh yeah," I proudly assured her. "I make my mother's recipe."

It was one of the ways I enjoyed remembering my mom. Though Nichole couldn't have known it, the experience of losing my mother had set the stage for me to fall in love with her son. The memory of my mother's death and burial, the meaning and dignity and respect of it, is what I'd wanted so much for Nicholas. For Zachary. For Tim. My mother continued to live in my heart just as I knew Nicholas and Natasha would continue to live in Nichole's.

"Will you make me some dressing for my freezer?" Nichole asked.

Though it seemed an odd request, I was happy to oblige.

Nicholas's original gown had finally arrived in the mail, and the "Thanksgiving dressing" visit would be the perfect excuse to surprise Nichole by giving her the gorgeous garment. The gown was pure white linen. On the chest was a crocheted embellishment featuring an appliqued cross with the word "Love" embroidered in blue. Before presenting it to Nichole, I had the name "Natasha" added in pink thread, stitched in a feminine script. A few days later, when we met, it actually opened the door to a sacred opportunity to share Jesus's great love and forgiveness, helping Nichole understand how Jesus presented her as spotless and pure before the Father. To my great delight, she was ready to receive grace, and we had the opportunity to pray together. I saw God redeeming so much.

After I met with Nichole, I dashed off to meet Addy, who asked if I could stop by her work for a moment. When I arrived, she handed me a cherry pie she had baked.

"What's this?" I asked.

"Tim loved cherries," she explained, "and I wanted to make this for your family."

"Thank you! It looks delicious!"

Addy told me that on Thanksgiving she would take her pie to Tim's grave to eat there.

As we parted she hugged me good-bye and then asked, with no presumption, "May I call you on Thanksgiving?"

Her request touched my heart. When I first learned of Nichole's Nicholas as "Baby Doe," he'd seemed so utterly and desperately alone. Since then, God had begun to knit together a most unlikely family—first with Addy and now with Nichole. Eventually they would come to form their own sisterhood independent of me.

"Of course you can call me on Thanksgiving," I assured Addy. "That's what family does."

For thirteen months I'd waited and wondered about the woman who gave birth to the baby I now know as Nicholas. I confess that the first day I met Nichole, her appearance and demeanor scared me. But as God allowed me to get to know her—as another mother who desperately loved her son, as a friend who loved fancy hats and Thanksgiving stuffing—God taught me that we were more alike than we were different.

CHAPTER 5

Unforgettable Dixie January

Early on when Alfie inquired whether or not my "organization" would care for Baby Zachary, I was taken aback. There was no organization. No board of directors. No mission statement. At that time I heard only God's gentle whisper: "I'm in this with you. I am all you need." I heard the same soothing refrain when Nicholas was identified. And when Tim's family needed a headstone. As I cared for each child, the little I was able to discern about the Spirit-led adventure unfolding before me was that God was calling me to offer dignity in death to children who otherwise would not receive it.

But Alfie's inquiry drove me to ask God, "Is this just you and me, or is it something bigger?"

As God and I talked, I did sense that a ministry greater than me was being born. A collaborative effort of providers and volunteers. To be most effective, my yes to God depended on a lot of other people's yeses. With the eyes of my heart, what was unfolding looked to me like the body of Christ in motion, living out the kingdom Jesus ushered in.

As I prayed for Baby Doe during the months before Nicholas's body was identified, a song had pulsed in my heart and mind called *He Knows Your Name*. And as God continued to open new doors, to care for other families, those four words felt like a holy seal on the burgeoning ministry. Over the life of each child, God continued to sing, "I will give them an everlasting name that will endure forever" (Isaiah 56:5). Because each life was so intimately known to God, each was precious and each was worth honoring. And though I still had no interest in creating an organization, He Knows Your Name became the ministry umbrella that would shelter wherever God led. It still functioned very organically, as I continued to move in response to God's unlikely invitations, but identifying the growing ministry as He Knows Your Name gave others a handle to understand what was unfolding before me.

While my ministry gained a name, my evolving understanding of where God was leading was about to be stretched. When I received a phone call from my daughter Anna, who was attending Baylor University in Waco, Texas, one of those new doors flung wide open. As Anna described a situation her community was facing, I was driven to my knees to ask God if the very unusual request had my name on it.

A BELOVED DANCER

At 11:17 p.m. on a Friday, Anna received a frantic call from Emily Mills.

Emily and her husband, Brett, are cofounders of a ministry—Jesus Said Love—to dancers in the adult entertainment industry. After leading worship at a conference focused on ministry to sex workers, Emily and Brett were transformed by stories they heard from former exotic entertainers. Specifically, they became burdened for these women that the church had marginalized due to ignorance or negligence. The seed that was planted at that conference in 2003 has sprouted and grown into a full-time ministry of club outreaches, social work assistance, education, awareness, medical education, child care services, and nutritional advocacy in several Texas cities.

When Emily phoned Anna, she reported that there had been an accident with one of the dancers they knew and loved. Emily and Brett needed Anna to be with their children while they raced to Hillcrest Baptist Medical Center.

The moment Anna pulled into the Mills' driveway, Emily and Brett pulled out. Children asleep, Anna waited on the couch, checked her phone, and prayed for a woman she'd never met. When Emily and Brett returned home several hours later, Anna finally learned what had happened. Dixie January had been learning to ride her fiancé's motorcycle in Waco, Texas, when she lost control of the bike and crashed into a creek.

She hadn't been wearing a helmet, and she died at the hospital.

Dixie was the mom of five kids and, as her obituary would read the following week, "She had lived a wild life but by the grace of God she was turning her life around." Though she supported her kids for years as a stripper, Dixie had become convinced—by Emily, Brett, and others—that she was deeply loved by God and that God was opening new doors for her. Two days after her accident, Dixie had been scheduled to be baptized at the local church she'd been attending. Her friends had been planning her baptism after-party for weeks. Then, on Monday, she would start a new job as a clerk at a clothing store. It was the fresh start Dixie had not thought possible. She was even engaged to be married to a man she loved.

Though tragically shortened, Dixie January's life had borne glorious witness to God's redemption.

JESUS SAID LOVE

Though God had been inviting me to care for children and their families, I understood why Anna called me in the days following Dixie's death. No one close to Dixie was in a position to finance her funeral. Her mother was without a home when Dixie died. After battling cancer with Dixie by his side, her father had died the previous year. As if purposefully marking his own transition with the calendar year, Mr. January had died on January 1, 2010. Dixie's fiancé wasn't in a position to pay the expenses Dixie's death had precipitated.

I'd not yet offered a headstone to the family of an adult, but I kept thinking about Dixie's children. These five little ones, ages two to thirteen, weighed on me. I knew they would need the opportunity to grieve the seismic loss they'd endured, both in the present and also throughout the remainder of their lives. I believed that a headstone honoring their mother's life would give them the opportunity to do that.

Anna reported that Jesus Said Love had requested donations for Dixie's funeral through their support networks. Apparently, donations had been coming in from around the world, from as far away as Poland. When Anna shared that they still needed more, I knew I wanted to get involved. I told Anna that I wanted to offer a headstone—for Dixie's children.

Jesus Said Love hosted a lovely funeral service for Dixie on Tuesday, November 15, 2011. Anna attended and called me that evening to describe the heartfelt outpouring of love for Dixie January. Emily and Brett spoke and shared Scripture. Coworkers and friends shared their memories of Dixie. Dixie's youngest, seemingly unaware, played in the grass. As Anna raved about the day, I realized that although the missions of Jesus Said Love and He Knows Your Name looked very different, God had called each of us to honor lives that others weren't recognizing as worthy of respect.

As the chaos around Dixie's death and funeral dwindled, I began calling funeral homes and monument companies in Waco.

A CLEAR MEMORY OF DIXIE JANUARY

"The woman who died is named Dixie January," I explained to Sharon, the administrative secretary who picked up the phone at Phipps Memorial.

Sharon had been rushing out the door when I called, and in the first moments of our conversation she blurted out that she regretted answering the phone because she had to pick up her grandkids from school. I offered to call back another day, but before she hung up, Sharon offhandedly asked me the name of the deceased.

There was a long pause on the other end of the phone after I told her.

Oh no, I worried. Maybe this woman knew her and I was telling her something she didn't know.

The pregnant pause continued.

"I'm sorry," I apologized. "Did you know her?"

"Well, not exactly. But that's not a name you forget."

I had no imagination for what Sharon would say next. Surely, I mused, she hadn't frequented the clubs where Dixie had worked.

Sharon both satisfied and piqued my curiosity by offering, "She used to come in here all the time."

What?

Sharon continued, "She loved to look at the books of headstone designs. She also loved bringing me her drawings. She promised that one day she would put down a deposit for a headstone, but that she just couldn't afford it."

What young mom chooses her own headstone? This was becoming more and more absurd. Then Sharon filled in the missing piece of the puzzle.

"She wanted a monument for her father."

Ah, that made sense.

I learned that after Dixie's father died the previous year, she'd been distraught.

"No one could afford a headstone for him," Sharon continued. "She just always said she dreamed of designing his headstone and purchasing it for him. She really wanted that."

"I can't believe I am finding this out. Do you happen to have a design of what she gave you on your computer?"

"I do. I have it right here. I'll email it to you."

DIXIE'S LAST WISH

I knew that Brett and Emily, who'd known Dixie for years, had cared for her when her father had been dying. They helped, to the degree they were able, with his funeral service. They were very close to her but had no idea that she had so desperately wanted for him to have a headstone. I asked Brett if he'd be willing to inquire with Dixie's mom, fiancé, and friends to see if they'd been aware of this.

They hadn't known. Not one realized she'd been doodling designs on cocktail napkins and grocery receipts, and visiting Phipps Memorial.

"You uncovered her last wish," Brett marveled.

Dixie and her father, George, were buried beside one another. With the designs Sharon sent, I was able to create headstones for both George and Dixie. George's headstone featured a fisherman hooking a trout, because he'd loved fishing. His birthdate revealed he'd been just twenty the January his girl was born. Dixie's headstone featured an angel, head bowed in prayer, as well as several butterflies signaling the new life Dixie had found.

Until Dixie and George, I'd only served children who needed to be honored with dignity in death. Despite Alfie's assumption that I ran the kind of organization that had a mission statement and a strategic five-year plan, I was still weighing each opportunity and asking God for a "go" or a "no." One of the reasons that Dixie's headstone had been a "go" was because it was for her children. Whether or not there was a head-stone, grief had become her children's lot. And I knew that grief wasn't something that would simply dissolve if unattended. It needed to be processed. If they were to heal, Dixie's children needed to face what they had endured. And God was continuing to teach me—through Nichole and Addy and others—that in the void of death, the unlikely way to new life was not to dodge suffering but to bear it. Even children needed the opportunity to face death's sting and discover, there, God's presence and comfort. My prayer was that the monuments, which had been erected for their mother and for their grandfather, would provide a small oppor-tunity for Dixie's children to heal.

A few months after the headstones had been set, I was visiting my children in Texas and stopped by the cemetery to see the stones. I smiled when I saw Dixie's and George's, side by side. George's headstone was scattered with a smattering of silk flowers and Dixie's was overflowing with flowers and bouquets. I quietly prayed that some represented a visit from the children who were missing their mom, a woman whose life had been twice redeemed: once on earth and now once in heaven.

Participating with Jesus Said Love in honoring the lives of Dixie and George convinced me that God's inscrutable plans and purposes couldn't always be captured by a tight mission statement. If I had clung to a missional rigidness about honoring only infants and children, I would have missed out on the beautiful celebration of two generations of family that God had so tenderly orchestrated. Because nothing about what God was up to could be captured, bottled, or boxed, I was learning to seek his face for each step of the journey.

The He Knows Your Name umbrella had just gotten a little bigger.

STANDING TOGETHER UNDER THE BIG UMBRELLA

The ways God would open up new opportunities was expanding as well. I'd discovered Nicholas's need on the evening news. Alfie had let me know about Zachary and had introduced me to Addy. That impulse, someone noticing a need and sharing it with me, is one of the ways God began to open new doors of possibility. A friend or church member would watch a news segment about a need or read an article in the newspaper and send the information my way. Sometimes these referrals felt a bit like a young adult who drops a pile of dirty laundry in front of the washing machine, expecting mom to take care of it. When someone would send me a link, with no apparent interest in being part of the unfolding redemptive story, part of me wondered, "Why don't *you* respond? Why don't you ask what God wants *you* to do?"

This is why I was particularly blessed that my Anna had seen a need and wanted to respond. When she'd moved to Texas five months earlier, I was still harboring concerns about her health and well-being. If Anna was struggling, so far away, would I even know? But when she reached out on Dixie's behalf, God gave me a precious glimpse into the ways he was healing Anna. God showed me a deep place of compassion and tenderness, assuring me that he was bringing her back from the brink of death. Just as these opportunities to minister among the brokenhearted were ministering to my own grieving heart, I could see how advocating for those in need was now also shaping and strengthening my precious daughter.

What blessed and encouraged me most was seeing the ways others were discovering their own unique responses. Nichole and Addy were blossoming in their care for other moms. Caroline was involved with He Knows Your Name in Indianapolis and was becoming precious to Addy. And whenever I needed an arm for support, lips to pray, or a shoulder to cry on, Steve was ready to step in.

When I received an email from my sister Julie about a baby in Racine, Wisconsin, who needed a headstone, I didn't know which kind of "referral" it would be. Was Julie responding to God's gentle whisper or dodging it? Her message read simply, "I think you'll be interested in this."

She was right. I was.

The article's opening line read, "The Racine County Sheriff's Office is seeking donations on behalf of a baby named Marianna that was born prematurely and died shortly after birth. The child was buried but does not have a headstone."[7] Baby Marianna's mother, at fourteen, had been beaten and raped by a man she was dating. Baby Marianna's conception was a result of that rape, and her death was the result of her mother being beaten later in pregnancy. The attacker had gone to prison, but this precious girl—I'll call her "Cammie"—did not have the resources to honor her child with a headstone. An attentive detective at the sherrif's office, clearly cut from the same caring public servant cloth as kind-hearted Alfie, was soliciting donations to honor Baby Marianna.

God had used Julie to open a new door.

Though I would not have blamed Julie for sharing the link and moving on, she didn't. In fact, after I finally traveled to Racine to dedicate Marianna's headstone, my sisters Julie and Jane, both living in Milwaukee, joined Cammie and me at the cemetery. On a bitterly cold day, the temperature just above freezing, they stood with this grieving young mom like two pillars of strength. With the wind whipping against us, I noticed Cammie wore only a lightweight jacket over her jeans and T-shirt.

As I began the service with prayer and Scripture, Cammie's shivering was visible and audible. Glancing down, I saw that this young lady was wearing sandals! My sweet sister Jane took off her outer wrap, her favorite black cashmere cape, and draped it over the shivering girl. Julie returned to the car and changed out of her boots into an extra pair of shoes she had in the car. She returned carrying fur-lined boots for Cammie to slip into. For me, the whole scene was a beautiful thumbnail of my sisters warming a hurting soul's body, heart, and spirit.

When Julie said good-bye at the cemetery, she asked Cammie for her phone number. That week Julie texted Cammie to ask for a list of her winter needs. The next time Julie was in Racine, she dropped off a load of gifts for Cammie: winter clothing, a *Jesus Calling* book, and a box of needed items that Julie had commissioned her Bible study friends to gather.

By offering the clothes off their backs and the boots off their feet, by remembering Cammie with gifts, my sisters were each faithful to step into something new with God. Willing to show up at the difficult place of death, they each came face-to-face with raw human need. And rather than turning away, they each chose to enter into a young mother's suffering.

Each of them said yes, in their own ways, to God's invitation.

Before I received that phone call from Anna in Texas, I was beginning to sense that God's unfolding calling would be limited to honoring the lives of children who would not otherwise be dignified in death. But through the opportunity to care for Dixie's family, God taught me how important it is to be listening, at every opportunity, for the leading of his Spirit. I didn't want to miss one thing God had planned! As scary as saying yes to God's voice was, it was no longer as scary as the possibility of missing out on God's adventure. So I continued to listen with open ears.

CHAPTER 6

Doodlebug's Lasting Legacy

March 11, 2012, I flipped on the evening news as I cut some veggies for dinner in my kitchen. It had been a full day: twelve moms and fourteen kids had met in my home for Bible study that morning, and I had run several errands in the afternoon. I'd just gotten home with groceries and was expecting Steve home soon.

On the news I saw lights from emergency vehicles flashing around a school bus and responders buzzing about the scene.

The evening news anchor announced somberly, "Two people were killed in a school bus crash today on South Emerson Avenue: sixty-year-old bus driver Thomas Spence and five-year-old Donasty Smith."

A five-year-old.

I shuddered, imagining the horrified mother who just received the news that she lost a child that day.

BACK TO SCHOOL

Earlier that morning, Danyelle Smith, a mom living on the south side of Indianapolis, had watched from the kitchen window as eight-year-old Erielle and five-year-old Donasty waited for the school bus in front of their home. It was Erielle's third year at Lighthouse Charter School and Donasty's first. Back in the fall, Donasty had been so proud to don her new pink backpack and march aboard the school bus with her big sister. Danyelle took comfort knowing her baby would be safe at school in the shadow of her sister.

It had rained a bit before the girls went outside, but the skies had cleared. When the bus slowed to a stop, Danyelle waved good-bye to her daughters. The girls had reported after the first day of school that their bus driver looked like Santa Claus, with kind blue eyes, a high forehead, and a full white beard. Danyelle had seen him a few times and Thomas Spence really did look like old Saint Nick.

The first step was a very high climb for Donasty, especially wearing a backpack almost as big as she was, but Erielle gave her a little boost from behind to help. On this day, Donasty had walked about ten feet down the aisle, but Erielle slid into the first available seat, the first one on the left, and called her back. Scooting over to the window, pulling off her backpack, Erielle made room for Donasty to slide in next to her. Erielle helped Donasty take off her backpack as the bus started back up and chugged off toward school.

Everything for the girls was running like a typical Monday morning.

BUS 439

The crash happened around 7:40 a.m., and throughout the day reporters pieced together what information they could. With all fifty students safely on board, the bus had approached an underpass on South Emerson Avenue that dipped under railway tracks. Lanes in both directions narrowed a bit as vehicles passed under the tracks with a walled embankment on the right and a concrete abutment on the left.

The bus should have slowed down to navigate the slim passage, but a driver behind Bus 439 witnessed it speed up for a moment, veer toward the center divider, and crash into the cement wall between lanes. A man in oncoming traffic saw sparks flying as the bus scraped across the abutment. Video on the evening news showed that the driver's side of the front of the bus had crumpled. Some witnesses reported seeing smoke billowing out of the vehicle.

Witnesses immediately rushed to the bus to help students get out. Both the driver and a child at his feet were unresponsive. The other children, weeping, were terrified. Many were able to exit the bus on their own, but it took forty-five minutes to extricate the remaining students who were injured or pinned. Ten injured children were taken to the hospital; four were admitted. At the time the news aired, two remained in critical condition.

After they were freed from the smoking bus, the uninjured students were taken to Lighthouse Charter School, where classes were dismissed at noon. Parents were asked to pick up their children at school.

The anchor reported that investigators weren't yet sure what had caused the crash.

It seemed absurd that I could be preparing dinner for myself, my husband, and my daughter while some other parent would have one less child at her dinner table.

GETTING CONNECTED

The previous spring I'd received a call from the director of the small charter school with a request to provide students with needed socks and underwear through He Knows Your Name. His number was still in my phone.

I abandoned my dinner preparations, dialed, and identified myself.

"Do you happen to know the family of the girl who died?" I asked, hopefully. "Or do you just know *of* them?"

"I know them," he confirmed.

"If there is any way you can connect me with that family and give them my number, I'd like to see what they need," I offered.

Willing, he agreed to do it.

And then, more quietly, he added, "Donasty was sitting in a seat with her eight-year-old sister, Erielle. Erielle saw her fly through the air and land on the bus driver, under the steering wheel."

PREPARATIONS

I received a call from the girls' mother, Danyelle Smith, two days later. She had chosen a funeral home and a cemetery. The administrators at the funeral home had given her a deadline by which to have the burial, but there was still some confusion and holdup about moving forward.

The family chose New Crown Cemetery so that Donasty could be buried with Danyelle's brother, who had been killed as a young adult. It was a double vertical plot, meaning that Donasty's body would be buried above her uncle's. Because the plot had not been paid off at the time of the first burial, the family now owed $900 for the brother's bill, before paying for Donasty's. They also needed to be responsible for the costs of the opening and closing of the grave. They didn't have the money.

Although I could already see that I'd be traveling during Donasty's funeral, I knew I wanted to advocate for this heartbroken family with the owner of the cemetery. I wanted to find a solution that would be a win for Danyelle and a win for New Crown Cemetery. I was confident we could.

Steve negotiates for a living, and his whole business philosophy comes down to two words: "win, win." If only one person wins, he says, it's not negotiating; it's debating. Everyone should walk away from the table feeling that there's been a benefit for them. There's a lot of integrity in that. I suspect it's something I picked up organically, watching Steve. It's what I have drawn on in conversations with the owner of this cemetery and so many others.

But I was also bringing something uniquely my own to that bargaining table: my mother bear instinct. Families like Danyelle's are living through unimaginable tragedy. What happened to her child, and so many others, was unthinkable. So part of my calling is to fight for these wounded ones. I have no problem being really firm when going to bat for them. I'm not mean about it, but I'm also not afraid to be frank and honest. I feel that protective mother instinct well up in my gut for these vulnerable families.

I also enter into these conversations knowing that healthy businesses won't suffer simply because they've helped to care for a handful of families who've endured sudden, tragic loss. The bottom line is that doing right by a family so tragically stricken with heartache is the right thing to do for the business, for the family, and for the community. Win, win, win.

I called the cemetery and asked if I could speak not with the administrator but with the owner of the cemetery. When I had him on the line, I suggested that rather than taking our business elsewhere—which, of course, I privately knew Danyelle didn't want to do—the cemetery could forgive the original debt and allow me to cover the expenses for Donasty's burial.

Win, win.

They agreed.

All along this journey, I've seen this principle at work: doing good elicits good. I've also noticed that sinful responses from broken people generate more of the same.

For instance, when tragedy is reported in the news with a filter that demonizes others, it breeds criticism and judgment. That was what happened before baby Nicholas's full story came to light, causing people to assume his mother must be a monster. Sometimes, as with precious Tim Bray, even the victims of tragedy are demonized. Seeking to make sense of a tragedy that is senseless, people assume he must have been a bad kid, a delinquent, or had a mother who didn't care. Anger, judgment, and violence breed more of the same.

But of course, the flip side is also true.

When you do good, you bring out the best in others. As a result of saying my little yeses to God, I've seen it time and time again. Strangers show up to support grieving parents. A ministry will message me on Facebook to provide gowns. Another will donate a charm. Another a headstone. And what thrills me the most is when people recognize a need themselves—a couple bearing unspoken grief for a child lost years ago, a mom laden with grief after an abortion, a sibling who never knew an older "phantom" sibling—and step in to help. I never expect for that engagement to look exactly as it looks for me. Maybe a man will simply honor a child's memory by asking to know her name. Maybe a woman will pray with a family as a mediator of God's active living presence. Maybe a family, in honor of a lost child, will work toward legislation like Indiana's recent Baby Box law, which expands safe-haven laws that allow parents to surrender newborns without fear of prosecution. In encounter after encounter I continue to see that working as an agent of redemption *elicits* what is good and kind and generous in others.

Graciousness multiplies.

A PREGNANT GRIEVING MOM

When Danyelle and I met at the cemetery, a week after her daughter had been buried, she stepped out of a relative's car looking very, very pregnant. She held the hand of Aubrey, her seventeen-month-old.

Though my heart is always heavy with and for these moms, the agony of Danyelle's situation exploded in my heart when I saw her. She appeared about eight months pregnant, just as Tim Bray's mom, Addy, had been. The stark juxtaposition of gain and loss, life and death, overwhelmed my maternal heart. I instinctively prayed that Danyelle and her new child would experience a bubble of protection around them from the emotional struggles she faced. I knew that a lot of moms who've lost an infant or young child consider taking their own life. In the wake of such devastation they find it difficult to imagine how they'll continue living. Even when they have other children who need them, the pain and depression can become so unbearable that they eclipse all else. I didn't know if Danyelle had or would experience suicidal thoughts, but I did know that I wanted to acknowledge and honor the new life she'd soon be welcoming.

"You're expecting," I observed, and then asked when the baby was due.

I knew, as she answered, that it was absurd to rejoice in the face of the somber circumstances which had brought us together. But I also knew that just as Donasty's life had mattered, this little one's life did as well. Danyelle shared that she was carrying a boy, due in just four weeks.

We found a seat inside the office and started talking about the design she'd like to see on the headstone. That was the premise of our meeting: business. But of course, as moms will do, she told me about her little girl, Donasty.

Danyelle had nicknamed her daughter *Doodlebug.* She spoke it with tenderness and delight, her eyes welling up at the thought of the girl who would no longer answer to it. Danyelle explained that when Donasty was younger, she doodled with crayons and pencils and pens. She drew on everything! She often had little art projects going around the home. Donasty, reportedly *always* happy, had been a breath of fresh air in the Smith family. Danyelle told me she was very active, very silly, and very loud! She had a big voice in a small body. She loved having braids in her hair. Donasty wasn't satisfied with a few beads on the ends of those braids: she wanted *stacks* of them. She also loved playing with dolls.

As I was learning more about Donasty, a woman about my age came in with a young girl whom little Aubrey obviously recognized. I introduced myself and found out the woman was Danyelle's mom. The girl, hair braided with white beads on the ends, was Donasty's sister, eight-year-old Erielle. I'd thought of her often, and couldn't imagine what she'd endured, having seen her sister fly through the air, dying on impact.

I turned to speak with Erielle. I suspect she was still numb from the trauma, as her affect gave no clue about what she'd recently suffered. In fact, her innocent presence felt like a relief in the midst of such a difficult scene. She told me about her school and her friends. She also liked to play with dolls, as Donasty had.

Then, intuiting the real reason we were all there, she breathed, "I'm going to miss my sister. Who else will I talk to?"

Though I hadn't felt particularly well-equipped or qualified to be sitting with Danyelle, I suddenly became aware of the layers of relationship between the three generations: a distraught grandmother helping to raise her grandkids, a grieving mother still trying to parent well, a sad and confused little girl. Every relationship was laced with trauma.

Lord, I silently pleaded, *what am I doing here?*

In a calm, gentle voice, God quietly whispered to my heart, *"Just listen and love. You can do this."*

Nothing about the assignment made sense. I didn't feel at all prepared, but I could do those two things: I could listen; I could love.

FIRST BLOOM OF SPRING

Danyelle chose a dogwood flower border for the headstone because Donasty had died in the spring and dogwood is typically the first spring blossom to bloom. Signifying resurrection, it often bursts into full flower near Eastertime. We also chose the font for her name and the dates she'd lived: August 2, 2006–March 12, 2012. After we made our decisions, the administrative assistant filled out the rest of the official paperwork.

With a moment to speak more openly, as Danyelle's mother cared for the two children, I asked Danyelle how she was *really* doing. She at last broke down, tears flooding her face. Overwhelmed with so much sadness, her pregnant belly shook with her heaving cries. It was the kind of grief mothers often try to mask from the remaining children in their care. I reached across the table and laid my hand on top of Danyelle's quivering one.

When we were finished, we all stepped outside together into the sunshine of a mild March day. After asking her permission, I laid hands on Danyelle and prayed for her. I asked God that all her children would outlive her, that she would never have to see another die again. Then, gently, I touched her bulging belly to pray for her son. As we were praying, Erielle came near. I put my hand on her back and blessed her spirit: "God, heal her pain. Direct her life. Reveal yourself to her all the days of her life."

We lingered in the parking lot a bit before heading to our separate cars. As we parted, I was overcome with two realizations. First, I couldn't believe I'd been allowed into such a tender, sacred time with a family. I knew that, though painful, this was also the place where real, raw, honest stuff happens. I also realized, *I've fallen in love with this family.* How on earth could that have happened so quickly? I've learned, since then, that our connection was amplified by the emotional circumstances, like the unbreakable bond described by soldiers who've battled a wartime enemy shoulder to shoulder. Danyelle and her mother had shared so intimately about the most tender places in their hearts. Easter weekend was just three days away and the three of us stood shoulder to shoulder staring down the enemy who is the thief that comes to steal, kill, and destroy. I was convinced that God had redemption in store for them, but I couldn't imagine how it would look.

I prayed for them in my car as I drove away from the cemetery. "God, I am trusting you for this. They told me their faith is so weak, and I'm lending them mine. We're counting on you."

I also prayed for myself. "Thank you, Jesus. I am honored to usher in the presence of your Holy Spirit with your leading and power."

I was amazed God had trusted me with this sacred assignment.

DONASTY'S HEADSTONE

In early July, I got the phone call that the headstone was completed and set. I called Danyelle immediately because we'd agreed to go see it together. When I asked her when she wanted to visit and dedicate it, she replied, without hesitation, "Now."

Danyelle, Erielle, and I met at the cemetery office where they hopped in my car to drive back to the plot.

New Crown Cemetery required bronze on headstones, and the dogwood vine really looked exquisite. To this day, the headstone dedication, with just the three of us, remains one of the most simple dedications I've ever done. We didn't have balloons to release. There weren't piles of fresh flowers over the grave. We were standing in thick mud. But it was a sweet time among the three of us, reading Scripture and praying together.

Afterward, I opened my trunk and pulled out a box I'd received in the mail the previous day. It was a gift for Erielle. One of Steve's business contacts had helped get the order processed quickly so that it would arrive in time for me to deliver it to her at the dedication.

When I first met Erielle, and then again at the cemetery, I was captured by her and by the enormity of what she had endured. Danyelle told me that she had become terrified of buses. Erielle wouldn't get on one anymore, and I don't blame her. Though I knew the gift I chose for her couldn't heal the deepest hurts in Erielle's heart, it was something I hoped she'd enjoy. Tearing off the wrapping, pushing back the tissue, she pulled an American Girl doll out of the box. The doll had dark skin, curly black hair, and brown eyes. She was wearing a casual outfit and also had pajamas with little cupcakes all over them. Erielle was delighted by the surprise. She named her doll *Donasty*.

I had to imagine there would soon be stacks of beads hanging from Donasty's head.

BACK-TO-SCHOOL STORM

We didn't realize, then, that our quiet time together was the calm before a back-to-school storm.

Around what would have been Donasty's sixth birthday, August 2, 2006, my phone and Danyelle's phone began ringing off the hook. As schools prepared to receive students back for the fall launch, news stations were ablaze with stories on bus safety. Both of us ended up doing a lot of interviews on the topic.

We also seized the moment to honor Donasty. Though school wasn't quite back in session, orientations were going on. Danyelle sent a flyer to the school inviting anyone who wanted to celebrate Donasty's birthday to join us for a back-to-school birthday bus safety moment at the graveside. She'd also taken a flyer to her workplace, where she worked as an administrative assistant.

I visited Danyelle's home one hot summer evening so we could plan the event together. As we schemed, Erielle played on the floor with baby dolls I knew had belonged to both girls. When I stooped down to meet her well-worn dollies, Erielle told me how she and Donasty used to play with them together: feeding the dolls, bathing them, and tucking them in to go to sleep. Danyelle, listening in, smiled and wiped away a tear. I could see in both of their faces that Donasty's memory was still very much alive in their hearts. It was almost as if they could feel her physical presence in the home where she'd been such a vibrant source of life.

As I drove home after our meeting, I continued to think about those memories that seemed to vivify Donasty in the hearts of those who loved her. At home, parking my car in the garage, I headed straight for my desk where I knew I'd find a memory of my own. A few weeks after my mother's funeral, my daughter Lauren, twenty-three, had sent me a poem that enlivened my mother in my heart the way Donasty's dolls did for Erielle and Danyelle.

Thumbing through file folders, I carefully pulled out my treasure from Lauren.

> I have an image of my Nana standing over the stove
> In her Holland home, in front of the picture
> Window that looks out over Lake Michigan.
> I can picture her tender movements
> Over a pot of boiling water as she poaches eggs for breakfast,
> Folding white over yolk as it rolls in the water.
> Every so often I stand

Over a pot of boiling water and mimic her delicacy.
The thrill of cracking a shell on the heated edge,
Releasing its center to transformation.

Like Danyelle as she remembered Donasty, I wiped away a tear. I was grateful for Lauren. Grateful for the mother God had given me. And grateful for the journey with Danyelle that was drawing me even deeper into God's healing of my own heart.

On Saturday morning, August 2, not knowing who would come to the birthday gathering, Danyelle and I showed up at Donasty's grave and waited.

New Crown Cemetery is flat and treeless. At about nine forty-five we saw, across a sea of graves, cars and vans and taxis begin to flood the gates. They just kept rolling in: Donasty's extended family, the families of rising first graders who'd known Donasty, teachers from the school, Danyelle's coworkers, and others who just wanted to lend support all showed up. As more and more cars streamed into the cemetery, the mantra from the movie *Field of Dreams* lodged in my mind: "If you build it, they will come." I hadn't imagined such a turnout and I really couldn't believe what I was seeing.

The heat was sweltering. At a quarter past the hour, cars were still coming. I popped open the trunk of my car, ripped the plastic off a few cases of bottled water I'd just picked up at the store, and offered it to whomever might be thirsty. In moments, two 36-pack cases had been consumed.

A cameraman from one of the local stations, Gary, was curious: "Did you expect all these people?"

"No!" I exclaimed, glad to say out loud what I'd been thinking.

"But," he wondered aloud, "you had all those waters . . ."

Though many of these details would come as a surprise to others, I'd come to recognize them as little signs of God going before us.

"God just does that," I offered. "*He* expected them."

Despite the smoldering heat, no one seemed impatient as we waited for folks to park and join us. A number of children and several adults were wearing T-shirts memorializing Donasty. They featured a picture of her on the front, and "Doodlebug" had been airbrushed on the back, with sparkles, as well as the same dates that had been engraved on her headstone.

It was almost ten thirty when we began the service.

After opening with prayer and Scripture, I asked all the children to come forward. There were a lot, and they crowded around me.

"On the count of three," I instructed, "I want all of you to say your names at the top of your lungs."

Their faces revealed surprise as they realized that such permissiveness meant that they weren't in school *or* church!

"One . . . two . . . three!"

They hollered a cacophony of names. I picked out "Erielle," "Jonathan," and "Tymeek." The rest blurred together into one joyful shout.

"Do you know that God knows your names?" I asked them. "Do you know that every one of your names means something to him? Do you know that you are written on the palms of his hands? Do you know that from heaven he is calling you by name and bestowing on you a title of honor?"

They might not have known what "bestowing" meant, but their eyes got bigger and bigger as they heard and understood that they were important. That *they* mattered.

"Every one of you will die one day and have a legacy," I explained, looking as many children in the eyes as I could. "Donasty has a legacy and we get to see hers now. I think Donasty's legacy will be that she changes the seat-belt law for buses in the state of Indiana."

That got a few "amens" from adults in the crowd.

I wanted each child to hear and believe that their lives mattered to God.

"God has called you," I assured them. "God has brought you here for a purpose, and you are loved by the Creator of the universe."

I shared the gospel with them and concluded with a prayer.

"Lord, in whom we trust, . . . we simply don't have the knowledge or perspective that we need to understand your purposes in the life of Donasty. So, dear Lord, nothing can defeat your gracious and redemptive purposes. Thank you that we have hope that you will comfort Danyelle and her family as they learn to live without their precious angel, Donasty.

Help them as they try to see this tragedy from a broader perspective of the Bible and make it clear that all of their pain will contribute to a far greater good that will continue into eternity. May all of us who love Donasty never lose hope in you and your works. In Jesus's name, amen."

I turned to Danyelle and asked, "Is there anything else?"

"Nope," she replied. "That was perfect."

Gary, the cameraman who'd watched water flow from the trunk of a Mercedes, marveled, "I have never seen anything like this."

Neither had I.

LASTING LEGACY

A year after Donasty's death, Danyelle and I decided to meet at the site of the bus crash to mark the anniversary of her death. Nichole and Addy came too, laying flowers and stuffed animals at the memorial site. It was beautiful for me to see how both women continued to be proactive in caring for other grieving mothers. We chatted about the women's lives and about Danyelle's precious girl.

From the very beginning, Danyelle had insisted, "I want a school bus seat-belt law put in place called 'the Donasty law,' in my daughter's honor." Danyelle was the one who'd immediately coined the phrase, "the Donasty law."

The week after we met at Donasty's grave, Danyelle and I each received a call from an administrator at Riley Children's Hospital who works on child safety issues. One of their new agenda items was seat-belt safety. We were invited to meet with a state legislator, a senator, heads of the hospital, and head of bus safety in the state of Indiana.

Though Indiana has, at this writing, not yet passed a Donasty law, Danyelle continues to speak out for bus safety as she honors the enduring legacy of a vivacious little girl called *Doodlebug*.

When Addy and I partnered to establish swim lessons in Tim's name, I saw her come alive in ways I could not have imagined. And now I was witnessing something similar as Danyelle insisted on championing a statewide seat-belt law in Donasty's memory. God was teaching me, through both of these women, about his redemptive purposes in the midst of tragedy. And just as they were finding healing by reaching out to care for others, I was too.

CHAPTER 7

A Life That Slipped
Away Too Soon

When I received a phone message from an attorney, I couldn't imagine why he was calling. I remembered that he had represented Donasty's mother, Danyelle, in a lawsuit against the bus company. But what on earth could he want with me? When we finally connected, he explained that he was representing a couple lacking the financial means to mark their daughter's burial place with a headstone, and he wondered if I could help.

In conversations with both the lawyer and Kelly and Mason—the parents of three-year-old Annaliese Obrien—I pieced together the story of Annaliese's last few months of life. Through their stories, I came to know another little girl with an unquenchable thirst for life.

SIXTY DAYS

For sixty days Child Protective Services had investigated the circumstances surrounding Annaliese's accidental escape from her grandfather's home.

It had been the first time Annaliese's parents had left her in the care of anyone else. The three were a tight-knit family who enjoyed being together. On most days, when Annaliese's mother went to work at a local sandwich shop, Annaliese's father, who was legally blind, cared for the girl. Mason loved being a dad and loved caring for Annaliese.

Kelly and Mason had left Annaliese with Mason's dad so that Kelly could go to work and Mason could do a few important errands. When Mason's stepmother, who uses a wheelchair, heard the door of their home open, she called out for Mason's father to catch Annaliese before she bolted. Before he was able to get to her, Annaliese had walked down to the corner of the urban block in front of her grandfather's home. When someone on the street noticed she was alone, they called 911. As part of the Child Protective Services' investigation into the event, they asked Annaliese why she had left.

She said she was looking for her mommy.

Ultimately the state's investigation would find no negligence.

FINAL MEETING

On the sixtieth day following Annaliese's unauthorized sojourn, Mason and Kelly were scheduled to report to Child Protective Services for their final meeting with investigators. After again leaving Annaliese with Mason's father and his wife, they caught the bus downtown to clear up the matter and put it behind them.

Playing in her grandfather's living room, Annaliese picked up an illustrated Bible. Thumbing through the pages, she pointed to one of the pictures, near the Jordan River, announcing that she wanted to go swimming. It was the middle of July in Indianapolis and the temperature had already risen to 92 degrees. Swimming was a great idea, but would have to wait for another day.

Annaliese was still thumbing through books when Mason's sister, Janie, stopped by her father's home to visit. When it was time for her to leave, Annaliese wanted to go with her aunt and Annaliese's grandfather allowed it.

Mason and Kelly returned about an hour later to pick up their daughter. Not only was the couple surprised to discover their daughter wasn't where they'd left her, the news that she'd left with Janie was disconcerting for Kelly, who had a strained relationship with Mason's sister. As they were discussing the troubling situation with Mason's father, the phone rang. Janie, upset, called her father to say that she couldn't find Annaliese. Distraught, Kelly and Mason rushed over to her apartment.

WANDERLUST

Just over an hour earlier, on the way back to her home with Annaliese, at around three thirty in the afternoon, Janie Obrien had stopped to pick up some food from a restaurant. After she and Annaliese returned home and finished eating, Janie laid down to rest while Annaliese played nearby. When she awoke, Annaliese was gone and the door to Janie's apartment was ajar.

When she realized Annaliese wasn't in the apartment, Janie began to call out for the girl. Growing anxious, Janie began knocking on the doors of a few neighbors, hoping they'd seen her. When Annaliese didn't turn up, Janie peeked outside, scanning the parking lot. Annaliese had been wearing a pink T-shirt and plaid shorts. Not spotting her small frame, Janie phoned her father and also called the Indianapolis police, who arrived within ten minutes.

After obtaining a description of the girl, the police began knocking on more doors and searching in and around the building. Concerned neighbors began to join the search.

SOMETHING PINK

By this time, a frantic Mason and Kelly had also arrived. Kelly, noticing one officer with a dog trained to track a human scent, was terrified. Family and neighbors and officers searched for the little girl.

At approximately four thirty, from a second-story balcony, one of the neighbors spotted "something pink" floating in the retention pond on the far side of the parking lot. Calling out for help, the neighbor directed an officer who splashed into the pond to pull the girl out. Police called for an ambulance and began performing mouth-to-mouth resuscitation. When paramedics arrived, they took over as they rushed her into the ambulance and to Community East Hospital.

Annaliese was pronounced dead when she arrived.

Though no one knows exactly how Annaliese's final minutes unfolded, bits can be pieced together. Annaliese would have pushed open a heavy exterior door that led outside. The door fed into a large parking lot. The spaces closest to the building were occupied, but those farther from the building were vacant. Annaliese then walked across a piping hot parking lot, sizzling in the summer heat, the blacktop hot on her tender feet. Spotting a pond adjacent to the complex, Annaliese walked through a yard of tall grass toward a steep rocky bank beside the pond.

Perhaps she wanted to cool her feet.

Perhaps she wanted to splash and play like she did at home in the bathtub, under the supervision of her parents.

Perhaps she still wanted to go swimming.

It's not clear how long it took Annaliese to make her way to the pond. It's not evident whether she meant to enter the water or may have stumbled down the steep incline. At some point on her journey, Annaliese had fallen in. Unable to swim, she drowned.

So much surrounding the tragic loss of Annaliese raised questions for her family and for investigators.

That she'd been barefoot had baffled her parents. They couldn't imagine she would go outside without her shoes because she *never* did that. She was so proud of her sneakers, featuring Dora the Explorer, and she never wanted to leave home without them. Mason says she loved playing with them and even carried them around like a toy! That she would have left her aunt's apartment without them seems, to her family, curious.

It was also hard to imagine that no one would stop a toddler who was unattended. I have driven past the apartment complexes where Janie lived and when the weather is warm everyone is outside. This vulnerable little girl had to have walked by half a dozen other people outside. Some were sitting in chairs. Others were talking on their cell phones. A few were usually smoking. How had no one noticed this little girl?

And how had she navigated her exit? The exterior doors of the apartment building, fireproof, were heavy. Somehow she'd managed to push one open.

Ultimately, though, none of those questions mattered.

Annaliese was gone.

To compound the heartbreaking loss, Kelly and Mason's extended family quickly began taking sides, some blaming the girl's aunt and others defending her. It was a pattern I would begin to see more and more as I walked with families through tragedy. Sometimes the conflict revolved around blame over the loss. Other times, when there would be a lawsuit or an inheritance, money would divide family from family. The pressures these families are under are intense, making them vulnerable to chaos, anger, and accusation during a time of loss. Annaliese's family was no different.

A FAMILY'S NEED

After making plans to meet Kelly and Mason at Washington Park East Cemetery, I realized that although I'd connected with several single moms before I met Kelly, I'd never sat with a *father* who'd lost a child. And Mason was a dad who was deeply invested in his daughter's life.

I've learned so much from Steve over the years about a man's perspective on entering into suffering. For anyone, it takes courage. But Steve has seen too many men run away from suffering, rather than embracing it as an opportunity for transformation, so he's passionate about encouraging men to bravely enter in. He walks the walk too: his own journey of deep suffering has taken him *deep* with Jesus. He's seen how God uses suffering to transform the children he loves, and Steve's tasted the fruit of redemption for himself. Steve and I prayed together that Mason would experience all God had for him in this harrowing moment.

Mason and Kelly and I met in the office of Marian, an administrator at Washington Park East. After losing her own baby, Matthew, years earlier, Marian was trained in infant loss and now volunteers at St. Francis Hospital among families who know they'll deliver a stillborn baby or a child who will live just a short time. She's certified as a family care specialist and now shares her huge heart of compassion through her work at Washington Park East. As I introduced her to Mason and Kelly, I breathed a silent prayer of gratitude for her ministry to grieving parents.

As we circled up in chairs, I observed the couple. Kelly had a kind face with a gentle smile. Mason was shy and had a very gentle spirit.

Kelly arranged a chair for him and made sure he was settled comfortably. They seemed to move in tandem—their physical closeness suggesting the intimacy they shared. Although he was blind, Mason had been an attentive father, protecting his little girl. When Kelly worked, Mason had been Annaliese's primary caregiver. Daily, he fed her, bathed her, rocked her to sleep. He played games with the little girl who became his special angel. Despite their physical and financial challenges, Kelly and Mason had provided a loving home where Annaliese thrived.

I listened to their heartbreaking story and felt the heavy weight of their grief. Amidst the tears were moments of levity as they shared about their daughter. They described a joyful girl who loved playing on her granny's porch and who lit up a room with her wide smile. They told Marian and me that Annaliese *loved* church. Several of her grandparents were leaders in their church, and her great-grandmother, Mildred, was an evangelist. Annaliese spent a lot of time at church and loved to pray. During the altar call, Kelly reported, people would walk forward and fill the aisles. Some, though, weren't able to make it all the way to the front of the church. Annaliese would reach out her arms to lay hands on people, praying over them from her spot in the pew. Tiny Annaliese, also called *Smiley*, was known at church for her confidence as a bold intercessor.

As Marian gently guided Mason and Kelly through some initial paperwork, I continued to think about Annaliese. Through her short life God was teaching me to welcome the gifts of children. Too often undervalued—even in Jesus's day!—God was showing me how the sweet spirit of a three-year-old had touched an entire congregation as she was allowed to pray blessing over people during worship and prayer. Had others hushed her up, or shooed her back, her natural gifts of compassion and intercession would have been stifled. Because of Annaliese, though, I began to see other children around me as irreplaceable agents of God's kingdom.

HOW TO REMEMBER ANNALIESE

When we finally discussed the headstone, I asked Kelly and Mason, "What should be on it? What would feel like something that was true to who Annaliese was, every time you looked at it?"

The couple paused to reflect on what image might best capture their beloved daughter.

After a few moments, Mason knew. Though he would never see it, Mason answered, "I want to know there is a pair of shoes on there."

Mason's face beamed with pride as he told me about Annaliese's delight in her shoes. When he would try to help her put them on, she insisted mightily that she could do it herself. I glimpsed his first smile during that visit, as he described feeling amused when she put them on the wrong feet and gently redirecting her.

I thought it was a perfect symbol. In the bottom right corner of Annaliese's stone is a pair of toddler shoes. In the top left corner, a kneeling prayerful angel. And a banner across the top of the stone reads, "Our joyful angel."

Among the families I work with, I began to recognize that many envision as an angel a child who has died. One of Annaliese's family friends wrote, in the guest book at the funeral home, "Gone but never forgotten. Our Smiley has gotten her baby angel wings and was sent home. We will miss you dearly. The storm will soon pass and the healing will begin. Keep your head up knowing that she is back in God's hands. R.I.P. Annaliese, aka 'Smiley.'"

CHRISTMAS LUNCH

Kelly was now a member of a club for which no mother wants to be eligible.

When Nicholas had been buried, I'd seen how much Addy's presence and support had meant to Nichole. And when Danyelle and I had celebrated the one-year anniversary of Donasty's death, Nichole and Addy had lent their tender, caring presence. Wanting to give some of these remarkable ladies a chance to know one another, and also wanting to shower them with care as the holidays drew near, I invited them all to lunch. I'd not known Kelly for long—in fact Annaliese's headstone hadn't even been set—but I knew she'd be blessed in the presence of these other brave moms.

As I planned for the luncheon, I solicited the help of some of my church and Bible study friends who'd been walking with He Knows Your

Name as its identity had begun to gel. Though some of them had not yet met this special group of moms, I knew these volunteers would love the special "Christmas elf" assignment I had for them!

I invited Nichole, Addy, Danyelle, and Kelly to a restaurant for a Christmas luncheon. We all dressed up in reds and greens and were feeling very festive. After a gut-busting lunch, I pulled out a little gift for Kelly. All the other moms had received charm necklaces with their children's names, wearing them that day with their holiday apparel, and now Kelly was receiving hers, engraved with Annaliese's name. She beamed as I clipped it around her neck.

These four truly were a unique sisterhood. As I watched them chat about everything from hair to earrings to fussing about their jobs or lack of them, I thought about my mom. She'd been a family counselor and her favorite book was *The Birth Order Book* by Dr. Kevin Leman. When I had my own four children, I began to see why my mom, who raised seven, appreciated it! And now, as I observed this new family that was forming, I began to recognize similar dynamics among the four "sisters." Nichole, the oldest, whose story had essentially birthed the group, played the part of the big sister. Addy behaved toward Kelly, the baby, like a slightly older sister might. And Danyelle, with her bright personality, was squeezed in between. Kelly, with an endearing sweetness, was the youngest and newest. All of them loved to "mother" her. By that time Nichole was actively sharing ownership of He Knows Your Name and saw herself as an integral leader, which she was. I'd catch glimpses of Addy looking for Nichole's approval as they discussed new plans and possibilities. That lunch was the genesis of the sisterhood. Although they may occasionally lose track of someone for a moment when she changes her phone number, these four have an unbreakable bond and are deeply loyal to one another.

In so many ways, these women were God's gracious gift to me in my own grief. Coming to know of and care for the children they had lost filled my heart with love. Joining them on their journeys took my eyes off of myself and my own troubles. Supporting them in their healing, and also in their efforts to bless others, gave me purpose I otherwise lacked. Though I never could have dreamed that being among the brokenhearted would foster my own redemption, God's gracious mercy was being poured out through these beautiful, unlikely vessels.

As we savored our dessert, I received a phone call. Peeking at my phone, I felt giddy inside. In that very sacred space I wouldn't have answered my phone for just anyone, but I suspected this call would be worth it. I excused myself and stepped away to take the call. When I returned, I was able to tell Kelly that Annaliese's headstone had been placed. She was so pleased, she quickly called to ask Mason to find a ride so he could meet us at the cemetery after the luncheon.

Before we left the restaurant, I asked the wait staff to bring out gifts I'd tucked away for each woman. They were large gift baskets that my generous "Christmas elves" had joyfully stocked with goodies they thought the women would enjoy. Each woman was just delighted!

After hugging and saying good-bye to the other ladies, Kelly and I drove to Washington Park East where we met Mason. Kelly's voice bubbled with excitement as she told Mason about her charm. She let him run his fingers over it, explaining that it had Annaliese's name and birthstone on it. Together the three of us shared a simple prayer, dedicating Annaliese's headstone. Kelly described the little shoes carved into the stone and Mason leaned down to feel them. He was clearly pleased. Rising to stand, Mason shared several more memories of the daughter he loved. I counted it such a privilege to come to "know" Annaliese as a smart, loving, vibrant little girl by seeing her through the eyes of her adoring father.

I offered the couple a ride home, and Kelly was animated as she described the luncheon to Mason, gushing about the other women, the food, and the gifts.

Mason, after all, had three new "sisters" too.

Until I met Kelly and Mason, I'd only cared for infants and their mothers. But as Mason grieved the loss of a beloved daughter, I was privileged to glimpse the heart of a father for his child: the protective spirit, the tender affection, the playful joy, the evident pride. In God's unfathomable logic, he'd taught me to "see" through a man who was blind. As God allowed me to see Annaliese through Mason's eyes, I could see more clearly God's paternal love for every one of his children, including me.

CHAPTER 8

What Are We Going to Do?

The weekend of Saint Patrick's day, Steve, Caroline, Anna, and I returned from visiting my dad in Holland, Michigan, for his eightieth birthday. Friends, neighbors, children, and grandchildren had gathered for a big, festive, green birthday party on March 17, 2013. One highlight was my nephew descending from the second floor into a packed house wearing his school kilt, from St. John's Military Academy, while playing "Amazing Grace" on his bagpipes. The celebration of my dad's birthday, the fourth since my mom had passed, was a bittersweet reminder of how well he was doing. He was driving to church each week and actively volunteering in the community. I knew he still missed my mom, but he was living a full, satisfying life. Living with congestive heart failure, functioning with a heart working at twelve percent capacity, he'd been admitted to hospice twice and had been kicked out twice! When he had his first heart attack eighteen years earlier, we never dreamed we'd be celebrating eight decades with him.

Steve and I were floating on a cloud in the front seat as we drove south to Indianapolis after the party. Suddenly, Anna and Caroline, in the back seat, became quiet and somber. As we neared the Indiana border, Caroline let us know that we'd all received a disturbing email from a close family friend. Opening up the email on my phone, I read it aloud to Steve as he drove. It was a hard one for all of us to hear and process. Realizing this unexpected rupture would impact our family for years, we spent the rest of the drive in silence as we each struggled to grasp what it might mean.

We arrived home around eleven that night. Dragging our bags, we headed for our rooms and fell into bed. Worried about this personal matter, both Steve and I tossed and turned throughout the night.

CALL FROM THE WEST COAST

Steve and I were up at five thirty the next morning, praying for our family and our hurting friend. I knew that in a few hours the young women I discipled each Monday would arrive with baby bags, Bibles, car seats, children, and all the burdens they were bearing. Though all I wanted to do was to crawl into a hole where I could weep and pray, I'd made a commitment to live my life honestly in front of these women. I knew I could be honest and trust them with my struggle, so I didn't cancel. I would simply be gentle with myself, and give them what I had to give.

When my phone rang at seven, I recognized Nichole's number. Not knowing whether she'd been up all night waiting to call me or whether she'd also woken early, I was shaking my head to myself as I answered the phone.

"Hello?" I answered, as much a question as a greeting.

"What are we going to do," Nichole began, "about the baby in the creek?"

Nichole's call took me completely off guard. It had been three months since our Christmas party and Nichole had begun a new job in Los Angeles, doing wardrobe inventory for *Dancing with the Stars*. What in the world was she doing calling me so early? It was five in the morning her time!

Tired, weary, burdened with concerns of my own, I had no idea what she was talking about. Was this a baby in Los Angeles? Indiana? Someplace else?

"What baby?" I asked.

As I had watched the amazing healing that God was doing in Nichole's heart, I'd seen her compassion for others who faced traumatic losses explode. It wasn't unusual for Nichole to call me about a story she saw in the news. Now the story of some baby found dead in a creek the previous night was pouring out, faster than I could receive it.

"Slow down." Taking a deep breath, I asked, "Where is this baby?"

The baby, she explained, was in Indianapolis. She'd seen the story on the Internet. Needing her to talk slower so I could understand, I instructed, "I need you to hold on a minute."

Nichole, understanding, paused to breathe.

Setting the phone down on the bed, I let my face fall into my hands. "God, are you kidding me?"

The needs of others—my family, our friends, my Bible study group, Nichole, this infant—were way more than I could manage.

What do you want from me, Lord? I asked silently. *How in the world can I do this?*

I felt God's inscrutable peace begin to comfort me even as I struggled to process everything that was coming at me. Nichole was in California. This baby had been found in a creek just twelve miles from my home.

I felt clarity come to my spirit. It was as if my burden lifted immediately. The sense I had from the Lord was, *"Linda, you know exactly what to do with that baby, and I want you to do it. The family friend you're worried about? I have her. You go get the baby."*

The encompassing sense of serenity I experienced made no earthly sense.

"Okay, okay," I told Nichole. "I'll call Alfie right now and see what I can find out."

"Thank you," Nichole breathed.

Before I contacted Alfie, I looked online to see what I could find about this baby.

BABY FOUND NEAR CREEK

While my family had been in Michigan, nestled around my dad in church on Sunday morning, a man who lived in Indianapolis on Gibson Avenue had been walking his dog when he came across an infant's body in Lick Creek.

As it had been for Nichole, Addy, and Kelly, the first news reports were already casting blame on the baby's mother. I confess I had my own questions, but had learned enough from my friends to steer clear of mom-blaming, even in my heart. With the best of intentions, a neighbor who'd been interviewed remarked that "this mother" could have dropped off the baby at a local fire station. The comment assumed the baby's mother was culpable. It assumed the baby was unwanted. It assumed the baby had been alive when it had been left.

The breaking news reported that "the coroner"—no longer an unknown person to me—was working to determine the infant's race, approximate time of birth and death, and, of course, how the baby died. Because the body had been ravaged by animals, even the baby's gender was unclear.

Since it had been almost three and a half years since Nicholas had been found in a dumpster, I now knew how it would go. There would be a criminal investigation that could take as long as a year or more. As I left a voice mail for Alfie, and alerted her via text as well, I figured that the case would be on hold as the requisite investigation took its course.

By 8:00 a.m., Alfie called me back. She confirmed most of what I'd read online about the baby. The "creek," however, wasn't really a "creek." The baby had been found in a residential area where yards joined together. There had been a lot of rain in March and the area where the baby had been found was a low-lying marshy area where water had pooled.

When a local resident let his dog out to run on Sunday morning, March 17, the dog headed straight for an object where two yards dipped together. The dog's owner walked over to see what his canine had found, expecting a dead bird or mouse, and discovered the body of a baby.

Before Alfie and I hung up, she asked me to call her the next day. I was beginning to learn that when Alfie asked me to call her at a later date, there was often something she couldn't tell me in the moment, but knew she'd be able to share later.

This was one of those times.

When I called Tuesday, just before noon, Alfie had studied the detective's report.

When she heard my voice, Alfie said, "I think this baby's going to be yours."

How could she know that? It had taken thirteen months before she'd been able to release Nicholas to me.

"How do you know this already?" I gasped.

Revealing only what she was professionally able to reveal, Alfie let me know that they would do a toxicology report and take DNA, but that she knew they wouldn't have the kind of evidence they needed to find this baby's family. I told her that I would move ahead by organizing resources so that I'd be ready if the child was released to me. I called Marian at Washington Park East Cemetery, asking her to talk to her boss about providing a plot for this baby. Because his assistant, having seen the story in the news, had already suggested this possibility, the pump was primed. He was in.

Alfie said she needed another week for the criminal investigation to take its course. She asked me to call her the following Tuesday afternoon.

As I stayed glued to local news throughout the week, reporters confirmed what Alfie had told me: there was very little evidence in the case. Throughout the week I held this little one in my heart. Though the baby's frail body had suffered decay, and the gender had not been reported in the news, I knew that if the baby who grabbed Nichole's heart turned out to be a boy, I wanted to name him *Moses*, which means "drawn from the water."

IT'S A BOY

In response to the news coverage, two different people contacted me on Facebook wanting to help. One offered flowers and the other offered burial clothes—a beautiful white, hand-crocheted gown with matching booties and a hat. All of this was in motion before Alfie was even able to confirm anything.

A week after we spoke, I called Alfie back about the case. "This baby is yours," she confirmed. "And it's a boy."

Ruth was the woman who had offered the gown. I asked her if she could personalize it in some way, and she trimmed it in blue ribbon and stitched Moses's name on the bottom hem. On Thursday I drove to Ruth's office, where she worked as an insurance agent, to fetch the gown. She proudly lifted the lid on the box that held her creations, showing off a gorgeous white gown, booties, and a hat. We had a great conversation.

As I was preparing to return to my car, Ruth asked, "Can I tell you something I've never told anyone?"

"Of course," I offered, taking a deep, calming breath so I could be present to whatever it was she might share.

"When my daughter was seven months old," Ruth began, "I found out I was pregnant again. I was so surprised. Not long after I told my husband, I lost the pregnancy."

"I'm so sorry," I said, touching Ruth's arm.

"That was two decades ago," she explained, "and I still think about him."

"Of course you do," I affirmed. I knew that gestational age could never serve as a reliable measure of a mother's grief.

Quietly, she added, "I named him Sam. I never told anyone, because I thought they'd think I was crazy."

I quietly suspected she was probably a bit *more* sane because she had remembered and named her son. I thanked Ruth for sharing her story with me.

"After reading your website and all the stories on it," she told me, "I finally felt normal."

Because Nichole had given me permission to share about her journey with Nicholas and Natasha, I shared a bit with Ruth about Nichole's loss of, and honoring of, her two lost children.

"Nicholas," Ruth repeated. "That was his middle name. Samuel Nicholas."

It felt like such a privilege to be able to stand with Ruth in that moment and affirm that her son's life mattered.

One of the principles I have witnessed repeatedly as God continues to open unlikely doors is one of multiplication. Every time a vulnerable life is honored, other unlikely lives are touched, as Ruth's had been. God uses the stories of the weak and powerless to shine light into the dark places of others' hearts, where they long ago hid some of their most formative memories. Sometimes, as with Ruth, the value given to a short or seemingly insignificant life is affirmed. In other cases someone realizes, perhaps for the first time, that a loss that had once been discounted as negligible—the death of a sibling they'd never known or a child who'd been aborted—was, in fact, deeply meaningful. Other times friends or family are inspired and equipped to care for those who have been suffering alone, sometimes for years. Without fail, God's redemption in broken lives continues to ripple well beyond the few lives He Knows Your Name can touch.

It is, I have discovered, the way God works.

MOSES PRINCE

The lovely Marian, at Washington Park East, worked alongside me to prepare a service for Baby Moses. As we discussed details on the phone, she encouraged me to choose a last name. When she said it, one word popped into my mind: "Prince." I paused to make sure, and indeed felt that *Prince* was to be Moses's last name.

Later that week I visited the neighborhood near Lick Creek where Moses's body had been found. Though his name had not been mentioned in the media, I made inquiries and discovered from the police report the name of the man whose dog had found the body. A friend and I drove over to the man's home to invite him to the funeral. When he didn't answer—perhaps wary I was a news reporter?—I left a note inviting him to the service. We connected by phone a few days later. Mr. Christiansen was conflicted: he was grateful for what I was doing, but was hesitant to engage further, still so disturbed by what he'd seen. I let him know when the funeral would be and he hesitantly said he'd come.

When I saw the autopsy report on the baby, I understood why. The report indicated the body was "not viewable." Baby Moses was twenty inches long, a typical size for a full-term newborn, but weighed just over five pounds. The details of his ravaged condition are unrepeatable.

SAFE HAVEN?

As Baby Moses's body was held inside his mother's body, during his final days of gestation, an inspiring documentary called "The Drop Box" was winning the Jubilee Award, the top prize at the Independent Christian Film Festival in San Antonio. The film describes the efforts of South Korean Pastor Lee Jong-rak's efforts to receive Seoul's unwanted babies. Constructed on the side of his home, the drop box contains towels, blankets, light, and heat to keep babies warm. When a baby is deposited there, a bell rings to alert the family and staff.

But Lee notes that South Korea isn't the only place with abandoned babies. Around the globe, babies are abandoned daily by mothers and fathers who are unprepared to parent them. Lee's work isn't unique. Germany, South Africa, Russia, Italy, and other countries all have versions of the drop box, meant to protect vulnerable children. In fact, every state in the United States has some sort of Safe Haven law in place allowing desperate parents to legally relinquish infants to hospitals, police stations, or fire stations. Indiana law now allows unharmed babies to be left with no questions asked.

A young woman named Amy Brown, in her role as the legislative liaison for the Family and Social Services Administration, was part of the team that passed Indiana's Safe Haven law in 2000. I have actually had the treat of visiting with Amy in my home. She explained that when another abandoned baby had been found in 2000, the executive branch was in session, allowing her and others to respond quickly in passing the legislation. The law allows overwhelmed parents to drop off a newborn at a police station, fire station, or hospital if they're unable to care for the child. Though Moses's caregivers didn't implement their right to seek safe care for him, Amy believes that the Safe Haven law is one important component of a larger solution. It gives women a choice. And yet today, bound by fear and shame, parents are still allowing their babies to die rather than entrusting them to reliable guardians.

Recognizing that more needed to be done, activists successfully lobbied Indiana lawmakers to install a version of Pastor Lee's "drop box" that would anonymously receive infants in need of care without the potentially shameful stigma of being identified by medical, rescue, or law enforcement professionals. In the process, I testified before the Indiana State Legislature to prevent something like Baby Moses's abandonment from ever happening again. Safe Haven Baby Boxes are now being installed in fire stations across our state.

COMMUNITY IMPACT

One dimension of Moses's story created a dynamic I hadn't encountered before. The gruesome circumstances around his discovery deeply affected the close-knit residential area near Lick Creek. This is the kind of community where neighbors know one another and help each other out when they can. The news came as a blow to many. Marian, my contact and friend at Washington Park East Cemetery, and her husband attended Faith United Methodist Church, located in the neighborhood where Moses had been found. She told me this congregation was deeply invested, praying for the situation every day. Just as people throughout the city were rattled when Nicholas was found in an industrial dumpster in an office park, Moses's discovery was, for nearby neighbors in this residential neighborhood, very personal.

Moses's death was also personal to me, as all of them were. But unlike those who had parents who cared so deeply for them, like Nicholas or Annaliese, Moses—who I'd adopted as my own in death—was *my son*. I was so glad that Steve, Anna, and Caroline could all be with me as he was laid to rest. When we arrived at the funeral home to follow their vehicle to the cemetery, I noticed that Indiana Funeral Care hadn't chosen their minivan to transport Moses, but had loaded his casket into the classiest coach they owned. Baby Moses Prince was going to ride in regal style to Washington Park East Cemetery. When we arrived, a line of cars was already assembled near the grave. Marian and her husband, Joe, had picked up fifty balloons I'd ordered, and as we pulled up I saw them distributing the balloons to those who'd gathered.

Steve met funeral director David Ring at the back of the coach and carried Baby Moses's little casket to the stand beside the grave. The flowers that had been delivered to the funeral home were brought out and positioned as well. When everything seemed ready, I invited everyone to gather around the site, and we began.

As much as any service I'd conducted prior or since, this one was really *for* the local community who'd been hit so hard by the tragedy. I invited the Reverend Manifold, the pastor at Faith United Methodist, to participate in the graveside service and to invite any church members who'd like to attend. Feeling almost like divine serendipity, it was held on Saturday, March 30, the day before Easter. About thirty-five people gathered, some were from Faith United Methodist, some were nearby neighbors, and some were from the He Knows Your Name family. As I welcomed everyone, I caught a glimpse of both Mr. Christiansen, who'd found Moses's body, and kind Ruth, who'd stitched Moses's burial clothing. I now knew she must have held her own son in her heart as she leaned over her sewing machine carefully stitching the outfit.

Although Nichole had been working in California, she desperately wanted to return for the funeral service to honor Moses's life. She had mentioned Moses's story to an actor and comedian who was one of the celebrity contestants on *Dancing with the Stars*, and he bought her a plane ticket so that she could participate. Reverend Manifold opened the service by offering a prayer for the mother of Baby Moses. It was such a stretch of the mind to imagine what she could possibly have endured, and of course I realized we might not ever really know. On that aptly timed Easter eve, I offered a reflection that met us where we all found ourselves that day—in the void between Friday's death and Sunday's resurrection.

Throughout that Easter season I was hearing the biblical narrative differently than I'd ever heard it before. In the narration of Jesus's final hours, Matthew, Mark, and John all tell the story of a man named Joseph of Arimathea. A member of the Jewish Sanhedrin, he was a wealthy man and he was also a private follower of Jesus. When he boldly approached Pontius Pilate to request the body of Jesus for burial, his secret was out. After Pilate granted the request, Joseph purchased fine linen and went to the cross to remove Jesus's body with Nicodemus. After applying spices and wrapping it for burial, the two men took Jesus's body to a man-made cave, which was actually the tomb that had been reserved for Joseph's own eventual burial.

I was particularly struck by the way in which Joseph chose not to flee from the suffering of Jesus, but to enter in. The temptation in the first century was the same one we face today: to avoid pain, to avoid suffering, and, ultimately, to avoid death. But of course, there was no local funeral home in the first century! People's families and friends were the ones who prepared bodies for burial. Joseph and also his friend Nicodemus were willing to touch Jesus's torn and bloodied body. They looked on his nakedness. They entered into the tomb. In Jesus's deepest suffering and humiliation, they were *with* him and *for* him. By reflecting the near presence of God to those who suffer, Joseph shows us what it looks like.

When my friend Jennifer sang "By Name I Have Called You," the words were vivified in a new way as they were sung over Moses's coffin. Fresh life and meaning were breathed into the lyrics that were so closely mirrored in He Knows Your Name's mission from the Scripture it was founded on, Isaiah 45:4: "For the sake of Jacob my servant, of Israel my chosen, I summon you by name and bestow on you a title of honor, though you do not acknowledge me." The same was true as Nichole, holding my Bible, read a passage from Psalm 139. The words being spoken from the lips of a mother who longed for and loved her son, over the body of a seemingly unwanted baby, were powerful. Measured, with thoughtfulness and emotion, Nichole read the words that leapt off the pages as they never had before. As they fell from her lips, the psalm rang with fresh meaning:

> For you created my inmost being;
>> you knit me together in my mother's womb.
> I praise you because I am fearfully and wonderfully made;
>> your works are wonderful,
>> I know that full well.
> My frame was not hidden from you
>> when I was made in the secret place,
>> when I was woven together in the depths of the earth.
> Your eyes saw my unformed body;
>> all the days ordained for me were written in your book
>> before one of them came to be.
> How precious to me are your thoughts, God!
>> How vast is the sum of them!
> Were I to count them,
>> they would outnumber the grains of sand—
>> when I awake, I am still with you.
>
> (Psalm 139:13–18)

I am still with you.

The words of the psalmist, spoken through Nichole's trembling lips, represented the voice of Moses. And also the voice of Nicholas.

Anna, my precious daughter who'd been close to death's door herself, closed the service in prayer, revealing a depth of faith well beyond her twenty-one years. Marveling at her poise, maturity, and health, my spirit praised God for the gracious healing I'd seen him do in Anna's heart. In Nichole's heart. In my own.

LIFTED TO THE HEAVENS

As the service concluded, Nichole invited everyone to step out from under the tent and tree cover to release the balloons we'd been holding in Moses's honor, similar to what we'd done for Nicholas. Necks craned, we watched the balloons ascend to the heavens as Jennifer sang a worship song. It was yet another reminder that Moses was now held in the loving arms of Jesus.

Several of us returned to the grave as Moses's casket was lowered into the ground. Anna lifted a bouquet so that people could pull a flower out and toss it on top of the casket, which had been laid inside the vault.

As folks began to disperse, Nichole and I crossed the Babyland area of the cemetery toward Nicholas's grave and laid a flower down on top of it. Then we did the same for Zachary.

One of the reporters who attended the service grabbed Jennifer, who had sung so beautifully, and interviewed her. I listened in as she described a conversation she'd had at home with her boys, ages five and eight. Earlier that morning, as they were suiting up for soccer games, she told them she was coming to sing at this service for a baby who'd been abandoned. Her youngest, with tears in his eyes, said, "Mom, we could have taken care of him." Out of the mouth of a babe came the sentiment so many of us felt.

From the corner of my eye, I noticed someone approaching me with some hesitancy. It was Mr. Christiansen, the man who'd found Baby Moses. I was so delighted he'd come. Seeming a bit shy, he let me know that it had been healing for him to be at the funeral. He was curious to know if I'd learned the cause of death. I hadn't, but promised I'd let him know if I did.

About a week earlier, when Moses's final headstone had been set, the cemetery had removed the smaller, temporary, five-pound marble stone. It had been weighing on my heart to give it to Mr. Christiansen. In my mind's eye I could see it laying in his yard as a memorial to Moses. This was my moment. I dashed to my car and brought it back to him. When I offered it to him his face lit up. Smiling, he reached his hands out to gently receive it from me.

BREAK-IN

Eleven months after Moses was buried, I saw a segment on the news about the congregation who'd prayed for him and who'd stood by him as he was laid to rest—Faith United Methodist Church.

It had been a rough winter, and the church had canceled services for several weeks in a row due to the harsh weather conditions. When the weather cleared enough for Reverend Manifold to trudge back into the building, he noticed a broken window in the office. Searching the premises, he found that some candlesticks had been taken, and also a very special jar.

As far as plastic Costco-size animal cookie jars go, it was as special as they get.

For months, the children of the church had been collecting coins— ones they'd earned as allowance, ones they'd collected from neighbors, ones they'd talked their parents out of—to donate to a mission offering. They had gathered three hundred dollars that had been designated for a little hospital in the Congo. Specifically, the funds would be put toward an addition for midwives to help mothers deliver their babies safely and teach them to care for their newborns.

The theft felt like a violation of something sacred.

Aware that the anniversary of Moses's burial was approaching, I offered to give a donation, in fact a double portion, back to the children of the church in Moses's name. The media continued to cover the story and I did ask that they show the website for the mission in Congo, Friendly Planet Missiology.

Moses evoked from me this little gift. His life also prompted Ruth to offer a beautiful hand-sewn gown and a local florist to donate flowers. Washington Park East and Indiana Funeral Care also contributed their services. Like every life, his was intended to have meaning and purpose.

I believe it has.

As I've seen in so many of these young lives, Moses's story continues to have a rippling impact on people he touched.

MOSES'S ENDURING IMPACT

In September of 2014, Steve and I were invited to speak at a day retreat for the city's coroners. Alfie thought it would benefit her staff if we spoke about He Knows Your Name. Many of them had heard bits and pieces about the ministry, but didn't know how those pieces fit together. When we went around the room doing introductions, one young woman, Amanda, was very emotional. Twenty-eight years old, she'd worked at the coroner's office six years.

After introducing herself, she gasped, through tears, "I worked with Baby Moses."

She began weeping. I went to her and just held her. She felt, in my arms, the way one of my own daughters would have felt.

Quietly, I offered, "I was told he wasn't viewable, but you saw him. I read your report."

Solemn, Amanda replied, "I did. And I'm still not over it."

I stayed with Amanda as others continued to introduce themselves.

When we took a break, Amanda confided, "I have never cried so hard in all my life as I did when I worked with that baby. My parents didn't know what to do with me."

This staff does one of the most emotionally difficult jobs I can imagine. And so much of it is unseen by those who want answers about their loved ones.

She added, "When he was released, and I realized he was going to He Knows Your Name, I was so relieved. Then I found out you named him."

It was an incredibly moving experience to meet Amanda, realizing both that I'd been protected from seeing the condition Moses had been in and also that she'd *had* to.

Before we left, Steve blessed this staff and gave them the big thank you they deserve to hear every single day. And three months later I popped into the coroner's office to hand-deliver a Christmas gift for Amanda. It had a hand-stamped charm, created by a woman named Sue Stevens, who—letter by letter—has stamped every single charm for me.

The front of Amanda's charm said, "Baby Moses." The back read simply, "We shared him."

She wears it daily.

I pray that it might symbolize for Amanda the important role she plays in the life of every body she touches. And represent, for others, the impact of every life, no matter how small. That's part of the deep congruity I hope that others will catch and grasp about this amazing, unlikely journey God has invited me into. When young lives are lost to abortion, miscarriage, stillbirth, or other infant losses, those lives *matter*, to God and to others. When precious lives that have been under-valued in society are lost—a thirteen-year-old African-American boy, a woman who worked at a strip club—*those lives matter.*

And as we're able to agree that the lives of Tim, Dixie, and Donasty *mattered*, then we are agreeing that *every* life that's been knit together in the womb of a mother is fearfully and wonderfully made (Psalm 139:14). It means that Tim's little brother in Addy's womb *matters*, each one of Dixie's precious children *matters*, Donasty's sister Erielle *matters*.

If the fragile life of Baby Moses mattered, which I'm convinced it did, that means that *your life* matters too.

And that is no small thing.

Though it wasn't an education I ever would have chosen, God had already allowed me to witness the ways tragedy ruptured the hearts of parents and other family members. Moses, though, was my first baby whose family was never identified; even to the grave his lineage remained known only to God. In a way I'd not seen before, the local community where Moses was found gathered around him, claimed him as its own, and grieved the way a family grieves. Through Baby Moses, God was teaching me that his redemption extends not just to children and their families but to the community who would claim them.

CHAPTER 9

A Baby Who Was
Never Forgotten

*I*f Christmas and Easter are the big holidays for pastors to shepherd their congregations, Memorial Day is the graveyard equivalent of "game time" for cemetery personnel.

On May 27, 2013, two months after Moses's burial, the staff at Washington Park East zipped through the cemetery on golf carts to be available to people wandering the premises and visiting the graves of loved ones. The tender, kind, wise, compassionate Marian, with another colleague, looped past one couple a few times before they stopped to offer assistance.

Over the years, Marian has developed an eye to spot those visitors who know where they're headed and the ones who appear more aimless. She recognizes those who walk with a purposeful step even into the farthest reaches of the property and those who need assistance. So she hopped out of her cart and approached the elderly couple to ask if they needed help.

"We know our daughter is here somewhere," the man reported with concern, "but she doesn't have a marker."

Jerry and Charlotte were white, in their sixties. Nothing they wore fit properly. Jerry walked with a limp, using a prosthesis where his lower left leg had been amputated years earlier. They both had rough, dry skin. Charlotte had some teeth, but clearly had had no access to dental care. Jerry was toothless.

That Marian had sought out Jerry and Charlotte was just one of many kindnesses I had known her to extend to grieving families. She continued to be a gift to them and also to me.

Jerry and Charlotte Laudig explained to Marian that their daughter, Melinda, had been stillborn in 1973. Over the years they'd tried several times to get her a headstone. They'd visited the cemetery office, met with Marian's predecessors, chosen a headstone, and put down a few dollars each time. But when they were unable to make subsequent payments, their contracts would expire and, eventually, they'd begin again from scratch. In Babyland, where markers are small, usually only ten by twenty inches, headstones cost around five hundred dollars.

Marian discovered, further, that the Laudigs' grief had been compounded through the years since Melinda had been born, because the hospital had not allowed them to put her name on their records. And of course, with no headstone either, it was as if their loved one and their loss had been denied. One thing I've seen over and over again is that hurts festering in darkness need to be exposed to light and truth if they are to heal. Loss must be acknowledged. And that acknowledgment often begins with a name.

MELINDA ANN

Sometime in the 1980s, Jerry persuaded the cemetery office to place Melinda Ann's name on the file. The small act had given the couple so much satisfaction. Now when they needed help finding her, instead of asking for "Infant Laudig" they could say, "Melinda Ann Laudig." Then someone sitting near Marian's desk would thumb through the filing cabinet and pull out her file to find the plot coordinates. Marian heard and recognized how important it had been for Jerry and Charlotte to see their daughter's full name written in marker on the side of a Washington Park East manila file folder.

On the Tuesday morning after Memorial Day that Marian called me to share their story, Melinda would have been forty years old. When

Marian called, hesitant, she confessed that she wasn't sure whether or not I'd be interested. It was a tone I'd heard before in Alfie's voice.

"Oh my goodness," I gasped, upon hearing their story. "They've waited almost forty years! Yes!"

While I never want to rush ahead of God's leading, I was sure that he led the Laudigs to Marian, and Marian to me. There was no question that God longed to touch and bless this precious couple who continued to grieve the loss of a daughter they loved. In fact, the reason I longed to serve the Laudigs, now each in their late sixties, was the same reason I'd wanted to make sure that Dixie January's three-year-old could one day visit her grave—to be given the opportunity to name and grieve a loss is to be given an opportunity to receive God's healing touch. I'd seen that beautiful healing begin to unfold in different ways in the lives of Nichole and Addy, Danyelle and Kelly. I was eager to see what God would do for Jerry and Charlotte.

Later that week, the Laudigs agreed to meet me at Washington Park Cemetery. In fact, on Friday morning we actually pulled up to the office at the same moment. Jerry was driving a huge, boxy, white four-door that was at least twenty years old and clearly on its last legs, sounding as if the muffler was about to fall off. Because the driver's side door no longer opened, Charlotte got out first and then Jerry climbed across the front seat, following behind her. As we greeted one another, I liked them immediately. We met Marian in the office and she led us to the spot where Melinda had been buried.

I listened to the couple describe Charlotte's pregnancy, how joyful they'd been, then the devastation they'd felt when they lost their first-born. They'd never stopped visiting her unmarked grave. Feeling the weight of their grief, I was more than certain I wanted to help.

Typically when I let a family know that He Knows Your Name would like to provide a headstone, they express some sort of gratitude. Some weep. Some say thank you. Some offer to repay me.

Not the Laudigs.

When I extended the offer to Jerry and Charlotte, nothing in their expressions changed. I was fairly certain they had heard me, but it was as if the words had not registered.

REQUISITE PAPERWORK

Marian led us back to the cemetery office and guided us as we filled out the paperwork. Both Jerry and Charlotte struggled to read the documents in front of us. Though I suspected they probably hadn't had a lot of education, their squinting brows also suggested that they both needed glasses. For the design to adorn Melinda's headstone, they agreed upon sleeping cherub angels with halos, holding a ribbon proclaiming, "In God's Care." The banner at the top of the stone read, "Mommy and Daddy love you." We carefully spelled "Melinda Ann," confirming the bittersweet day when she'd been welcomed and lost—March 11, 1973. Though they restarted the headstone process with evident enthusiasm, the couple became visibly anxious as we finished our work.

"We're not prepared to put any money down today," Jerry explained apologetically.

Perhaps they thought I was a representative from a monument company.

"This is something that I want to do for you," I offered, attempting to explain.

The blank looks on their faces showed that the offer had still not registered.

We actually went round and round about five times, with me stating that they wouldn't owe anything for the headstone and them repeating that they weren't able to pay in full on that day.

Because Jerry could see the costs listed on the invoice that had been prepared, he insisted, "Until I see that this says 'paid in full,' I won't believe it."

He was resolute.

After an awkward pause, Marian asked me, "What do you want me to do?"

Remembering the old rubber stamps I'd seen in my father's office as a child, I asked her if they might have one that said *paid in full*.

Marian left her desk to dig through drawers throughout the office in search of the sacred seal. A few minutes later she returned with a stamp and a red ink pad that had long ago lost its juice. Marian squeezed the last remnants of red ink from the pad and stamped the invoice PAID IN FULL.

Seeing Jerry weep as he held it, I knew he finally understood.

"IT IS REAL"

When I received notice that the headstone had been delivered, I made plans to meet Jerry and Charlotte at the cemetery to dedicate it. We'd meet at the gate, we agreed, and I'd follow them back to the site. When I arrived, I recognized their car, waved hello, and followed them. As we wound through the cemetery, I was amazed their clanging muffler was still hanging on.

After they slowed to a stop, they both tumbled out of the Buick's passenger-side door.

When Steve and I got out of our car, we noticed that two other cars had been following us. After I hugged Jerry and introduced him to Steve, Jerry explained, "The others are coming."

"What others?" I asked. Though I hadn't realized others would be joining us, I was learning to roll with unexpected visitors.

"My other kids," he explained.

Jerry had four living children, and two of them had come, bringing a few other relatives with them. As people began to exit the other cars, greeting one another, it looked to my eye like they hadn't seen each other for a while and were reconnecting. One woman stayed back in a car. I was curious, but decided to wait for the family to share.

Jerry introduced me to a man who seemed to be in his thirties.

"This is my son, Jerry Junior," he offered.

"Nice to meet you," I said, extending my hand to him.

Jerry Junior, who'd been chatting with a woman I assumed was his sister, seemed to be in charge of a five-year-old girl with long auburn hair, who'd been examining the headstone.

"Violet's hair is the same color as Melinda's," Jerry Senior reported proudly. "It reminds us of Melinda's dark red hair when she was born. We've often thought Melinda would have looked a lot like Violet."

Studying Violet's face, I realized what a gift she'd been to her grandparents.

While Jerry Senior introduced me to his daughter Charlene and chatted a bit more, Charlotte remained quiet. She walked over to the headstone where Violet was playing in the grass. After introductions, we all joined them there.

Though Jerry Junior, wearing his dirty work clothes from his construction job, appeared to have a tough exterior, a wave of emotion washed over him when he read his big sister's headstone. Through his tears he was only able to choke out three words: "It is real."

Charlene joined him at the graveside and began crying as well.

"We really *did* have a big sister," she said incredulously to Jerry Junior.

Their whole lives they'd heard about "Melinda," but somehow she'd never seemed real to them. They'd never met her. They'd never seen a photograph of her. No one else besides their parents ever mentioned her. And although they had no reason to doubt their parents, it had been hard for them, at some level, to believe she'd really existed.

The irony that a headstone made Melinda *come alive* to her siblings was not lost on me. It was a dynamic I have continued to witness in other families as well.

The dedication was simple: I read Scripture and prayed beside Melinda's grave. I also shared a brief message of hope, inviting those gathered to consider their own mortality. I welcomed folks to think about who would show up for them at the end of their lives and what would be spoken about them.

"It was courageous for you to come here today," I offered. "Melinda's legacy can help shape your life as you accept the truth that our days are numbered. The choices we make are what determine our relationship with our Creator." I also mentioned I would be available after the service to anyone who had more questions about Jesus.

I truly believe that it did take courage for each person to show up that day. Jerry and Charlotte had been preparing for that hour for years, but others had shown up to the service not because they were grieving but because Jerry and Charlotte had been. The family said yes to God's invitation to stand in the sacred place of suffering with those who suffered—to "weep with those who weep" (Romans 12:15 NLT) as Jesus did (John 11:35) and as we've been called to do.

Then I gave Charlotte her charm; it was round with an aqua bead with Melinda's name on the front and Isaiah 56:5 on the back. Delighted, a broad grin broke out across Charlotte's pale, round face.

NEW LIFE BIRTHED

Typically, after a dedication I'll excuse myself and let family have private time at the graveside. Because Jerry and Charlotte's family continued to engage me, I stuck around. As we were descending a bit of a hill to the cars, Jerry Junior approached me. His hair was a bit disheveled and his teeth, like his mom's, needed work.

"So," he began hesitantly, "can you get me one of them there stones?"

I didn't understand. Did he want a duplicate to remember his sister?

"Excuse me?" I queried. "I don't really understand what you're asking me."

Jerry Junior quietly offered, "I have a baby buried at another cemetery and he doesn't have a headstone."

I was beginning to recognize the pattern I saw emerging in these encounters. Often before I've finished with one situation, some new possibility has been birthed. In honoring Nicholas's life, Nichole was prompted to recognize and grieve her daughter Natasha. After stitching a gown for Baby Moses, Ruth was freed to grieve for Sam, the son she'd lost. And now Jerry Junior was seizing the opportunity to recognize the son he'd lost. I'd come to recognize these multiplications of God's grace as holy privileges.

"Well," I asked, "what's your little guy's name?"

He looked at me like I was a fool.

"Jerry," he answered.

Of course it was Jerry. I burst out in laughter and Jerry Junior joined me until tears were streaming down his face. I told him I'd be happy to do it. When he described where his son was buried, on the south side of town, I knew exactly whom I'd connect with at the cemetery, because it's where Donasty was buried.

When we got back to the car, Jerry Junior gestured at the woman who'd stayed behind in the car. She was sitting in the back seat with the door open.

"This is little Jerry's mom. We're not together anymore."

When he didn't volunteer either of our names, I extended my hand and introduced myself, asking her name.

She whispered her name quietly. But she didn't engage further.

In Jerry Junior I recognized a tenderness for the son he'd lost that was similar to the soft spot his father had for Melinda. Upon first meeting the senior Laudigs, I'd recognized immediately that honoring their daughter with a headstone was as important to Jerry as it was to his wife. As they stood beside Melinda Ann's headstone that day, Jerry's arm wrapped around Charlotte, he welled up with tears of joy for the gift they'd received. Jerry Junior had taken after his dad in that way.

Jerry Junior's ex did end up getting out of the car, but even when the family returned and was chatting together, she remained distant. I don't know whether she was unwilling to engage or unable. Though I usually connect with moms, my heart told me that this service would be for Jerry Junior.

JERRY JUNIOR JUNIOR

Jerry Junior's son had died more than a decade earlier, in 1999. The similarity to his parents' loss, both having visited unmarked plots holding the remains of their children, was heartbreaking. As we worked on details for the stone, Jerry Junior told me that his son had died of SIDS at five months of age. The timing struck me as unusual, because I knew most SIDS deaths happen in the first four months of life. It was also the same age Zachary had been when he'd died from what seemed to have been SIDS as well.

At the headstone dedication one chilly fall day, the service was very similar to Melinda's: Scripture, prayer, and flowers. Jerry brought a baby picture book, sharing photos of his son like any proud papa would. Many of the same family members gathered again. Jerry Junior's niece Violet was there, holding Charlotte's hand. She would grow up, I mused, knowing that her older cousin was *real*. I'd learned that Jerry and Charlotte spent a lot of time with her, helping with school drop-off and pickup, as well as volunteering at her school.

Long after the headstone dedications, the Laudig family, especially

Jerry Senior and Charlotte, continue to love me so well. They connect with me on Facebook regularly. They keep up with He Knows Your Name and participate in all the services I do. On Mother's Day, on Christmas, they send me texts telling me they love me. They call me their "angel."

While many in my community thought of what I was doing as selfless, God was caring for me through the Laudigs, binding up my own healing heart. Jerry and Charlotte's lavish affection for me makes me feel truly cherished. That's been true of so many of the mothers and families I've met. Again and again, as we share some of the most intimate moments of their lives, these families claim me as their own. God used the Laudigs, and others like them whom I never imagined I would know, to pour out his kindness as I continued to grieve my own losses.

Last summer, on my annual retreat with my Tuesday morning Bible study gals, I received a text from Jerry. It was a selfie of him grinning wide with a full set of teeth. It read, "I got me some teeth and you need to be the first one to see them." I replied saying, "You look like a movie star!" My life is so much richer because of the unlikely relationships God has allowed me to enjoy.

Beyond our care for one another, the Laudigs have become an integral part of the beautifully diverse tapestry of those who show up at He Knows Your Name services. During a recent funeral, several television stations showed shots panning the crowd gathered to say good-bye to two infants. It really was the most sacred glimpse of God's creation: old and young, people who lived comfortably and people of lower incomes, black and white and Latino. People with and without full sets of teeth. Truly, I think it's how God's church was meant to look! Some in that crowd, like Jerry and Charlotte, Nichole and Addy, had suffered their own losses. Others showed up to support the survivors—those known to them and those who were once strangers. What binds us all together is the shared conviction that every life matters.

Every single one.

MOVIE STAR

In response to an article in the paper mentioning the youngest Jerry, one reader sent me an email through my website:

I read the article in today's paper with great interest. I am a retired Indianapolis police officer and I was the one who did CPR on the youngest Jerry, trying to save his life. I have visited his unmarked grave many times. I thought if I could ever afford it I would give him a marker. I am so thrilled that you guys have gotten him one. I am now on a pension but would like to make a small donation to help offset the costs of the marker but neither the article or website gave the address. Can you advise, please?

Again and again, this is how it goes.

I continue to discover that every life, no matter how small, touches an expansive web of other lives. The shortest life is never without meaning and the rippling impact of this life endures for decades.

I applaud this officer for doing *something*. When I read the book *Kisses from Katie*, I was inspired by the author's clear message that each of us is called to do *something* on behalf of children in need. After rattling off a list of statistics about the world's millions of orphaned, hungry, enslaved, needy children, Katie Davis notes that 2.1 billion people on this planet claim to be Christians. "If only 8 percent of the Christians would care for one more child," Davis challenges, "there would not be any statistics left." She adds, "The truth is that He loves these children just as much as He loves me and now that I know, I am responsible."[8]

Honoring the dignity of every life isn't some special work assigned to servants like Katie Davis, who at nineteen moved to Uganda and eventually adopted thirteen orphaned girls. Neither is it relegated to organizations that can afford $500 for a headstone. God's call to accomplish small and large acts of love for the kingdom is for every one of us. If we fail to act because we believe the work is for others, we've missed the point. God calls each one of us to practice love in the lives of our unlikely neighbors.

The police officer who contacted me on Facebook is a great example. She not only wrestled to save Jerry Junior's precious son, but she continued to affirm, with her visits and with her donation, that his young life mattered. Seeing grace multiplied has been one of the most satisfying rewards of this journey.

He Knows Your Name recently received a donation from a family who lost their son about thirty years ago, at five years of age. His mother had seen him killed by a car in the front yard of their home. This family, who *had* been able to afford a headstone for their own son, sent He Knows Your Name a generous donation of $750. I thought it was an unusual amount. The same day, though, I received a request from a dad who'd waited twelve years to get a headstone for his son, lost to SIDS at five months. Because of the cemetery in which he'd been buried, the headstone was required to be bronze, which is much pricier than granite.

The price tag? $750.

I let the mom of the five-year-old know how her gift had been used and told her about the upcoming headstone dedication.

"I want to be there," she said immediately.

This flourishing web of giving and healing I've been privileged to see has been truly amazing. Every time someone offers a donation, every time I see a parent who's endured a loss step forward to honor his or her child, every time a brave soul is willing to open a window on a loss that has been shut away for years, I see God's healing hand. I have always known that healing was God's heart for the children he loves, and I've been blown away to see how generous God is as we open ourselves to his tender touch in the smallest ways. Just as it had been with Jerry Junior's big sister, and later with his son, God continues to redeem loss after loss.

As God had opened each new door, I'd been drawn into immediate, palpable human suffering. But when Marian introduced me to Jerry and Charlotte, God began to reveal his unfailing care for those who'd grieved a loss for decades. Whether suffering was fresh and raw or whether it presented as a long-held wound, scarred over but unforgotten, God noticed, God cared, and God longed to redeem. God's grace being poured out over the Laudig family exposed, for me, a new aspect of God's tenderness for all who grieve.

CHAPTER 10

A Most Fortuitous
Mylar Balloon

*A*s He Knows Your Name continued to engage with folks who were hurting, a friend emailed me an article about a San Diego family who'd lost the mother they loved.

Renee Finney's adolescent and young adult children had been living between their mom's home and their dad's home. One day in early May, eighteen-year-old Davion went to check on her mother and found her dead. Davion called her older sister, Karries, who came to be with her.

It was five days before Mother's Day.

After battling cancer for more than a year, forty-two-year-old Renee Finney was found dead in her Moreno Valley home. Renee was a single mom to three: Karries, 25; Davion, 18; and the youngest, a son named David, 15. With the family already stretched by Renee's medical expenses, the children had no way to provide their mother with a decent burial. On Mother's Day weekend, the children held bake sales, car washes, and distributed donation boxes to cover the anticipated expenses for their mother's funeral. They raised two thousand dollars.

One of their mom's dear friends had suggested that, in honor of Mother's Day, the children write notes to their mom, tie them to balloons, and release them to the heavens. The young adults thought the idea was juvenile but they knew their mom's friend had good intentions. So they dutifully tore some pages out of David's spiral-bound school notebook and poured out their aching hearts to their mother. On the evening of Mother's Day, Renee's three children rolled up their notes and tied them to a Mylar Mother's Day balloon along with a few other balloons. At eight thirty, they launched them, watching the balloons sail off into the darkening night sky.

One note that ascended toward the heavens read, "Hi mom, I miss you. I hope you come and visit me soon because I have questions to ask like why you had to leave me so soon."

JOURNEY BY AIR

Monday morning, Yvette Melton opened her front door to discover a cluster of balloons hovering on her front porch. Glancing down, she noticed something attached to the bottom of them. Picking up the balloons, she found the notes Renee's children had attached.

Yvette lived in Murrieta, California, thirty miles from where the Finneys had released their thoughts for their mom. It felt to Yvette like a sacred trust that they'd landed on her doorstep. When Yvette left that morning for her job at Color Spot Nurseries, she took the balloons and notes with her.

Arriving at work, Yvette showed the letters to her boss, Jerry Halamuda. Like Yvette, Jerry was intrigued. With Jerry's blessing, Yvette began to do research online using the names in the letters. When she discovered Renee Finney's obituary, she called the funeral home and learned that the family was indeed still in need of money for the burial expenses.

Jerry decided to take up a collection among the employees to contribute toward the burial. The words from Davion's letter that had tugged at his heartstrings read, "We know you're waiting up in heaven, but we don't have enough money to bury you yet."

Within hours, Jerry's employees had donated $2,024.

Yvette called the funeral home with the news and the director promised, "I'll call the family and will have them call you."

After receiving a curious call from the funeral home, Karries called to discover that the balloons she and her siblings had thought were a little silly had generated over two thousand dollars in donations. Karries was overwhelmed.

The media quickly picked up the story and reported that the family still needed to raise six thousand dollars. A link on the TV station's website directed donors to call Yvette at the nursery, and the phone started ringing off the hook. When she realized what was happening, Yvette created a GoFundMe page to receive the kindness of generous strangers. After watching the news on May 13, 2014, viewers responded. By Friday, an additional $12,648 had been raised. The generosity of strangers was another confirmation of what I'd so often witnessed: grace begets grace. Yvette's heart had unleashed Jerry's to give. Jerry had encouraged his employees to donate. Color Spot Nurseries inspired countless others. That the media had caught wind of what seemed to be a multiplication of loaves and fishes meant that Yvette's caring response rippled all the way to me in Indianapolis.

CONNECTED

When my friend's email arrived in my in-box, I called the Allen Brothers Funeral Home in San Marcos to find out what was needed. Because they didn't know how much money had been raised, they said that they'd have the family call me. When I hung up, I didn't really imagine that I would receive a phone call from the family in the midst of all that was going on.

I was wrong.

Within a few hours I received a phone call from Karries.

Kind and polite, she explained, "I am just trying to call everyone back who has called and personally thank them for caring." Wondering about my 317 area code, Karries added, "Where are you from?"

When I told her I was from Indianapolis, she couldn't believe that their story had traveled so far.

"Those balloons traveled thirty miles to Yvette's house," I marveled with her, "and then two thousand to my house through cyberspace!"

Knowing that she was now probably inundated with tasks to prepare for the funeral, I asked Karries what she still needed.

"It looks like money is coming in for the funeral," she explained, "but I don't know what the expenses are going to end up being."

Karries's experience was typical of most people who've not had the unfortunate experience of planning a funeral.

Curious, I asked, "Do you have any idea what you are going to do as far as a headstone goes?"

Although I was far away, I suspected I could probably work out the design and purchase of a headstone long distance. Though orchestrating a funeral from across the country would have been unwieldy, working with a monument company seemed manageable.

Already flooded with details to attend to, Karries sighed. "I haven't even thought about a headstone yet."

The burdens she was bearing were common to so many of the families I served.

"Well," I offered, "if I buy the headstone then any other money you get you can just put toward the funeral. Get done what you need to get done. I'll call you in a couple of weeks and we will make arrangements. In the meantime, I'll find the company we are going to work with and then we can Skype or do something to get a meeting going."

Karries was thrilled with the idea.

Before we hung up, I offered to pray with her over the phone. She agreed and as I prayed I heard her weeping, gasping quietly for air. Afterward, she let me know that she was finding her faith through this hardship in the ways people were blessing her family.

At the end of her own resources, Karries was discovering a new beginning with God.

DAVID'S INSPIRATION

All four of my own children were in their late teens and early twenties, as Renee's were. I hated what these kids were being forced to face. My maternal impulse was to gather them up under my wings. As Karries and I had the opportunity to talk several times over the week and a half before the funeral, we developed a sweet relationship. In fact, on May 23 we were talking as she drove to the funeral home to do her mother's makeup for the funeral. When she arrived, she parked her car and paused.

"I'm here," she announced, sobbing. "How will I go in there?"

As I hung up, my heart ached for her.

The following day was the funeral for Renee Finney. Juggling care for my dad, I wasn't able to attend. But I knew that Karries and her siblings would meet Yvette, who'd first gotten the ball rolling. *What an absurd commingling of grief and grace,* I mused. God was showing me that when a community vulnerably embraces death and life, strangers are knit together into family. I'd witnessed it in the unbreakable bond between Nichole, Addy, Danyelle, and Kelly. I'd felt it in the precious ways the Laudigs had claimed me as their own. And I was seeing it unfold once again as Renee's children warmly received Yvette and me into their hearts and lives.

Since Renee's death, fifteen-year-old David had been very quiet. Karries shared with me that she and Davion were worried about him. I told her that everyone grieves differently—some very loudly and some very quietly—but also let her know that I understood her concern. As Karries described the way that David had withdrawn, my heart *truly* understood, aching with the memory of Anna's difficult years. Just as it had been horrific for Renee's children to see her physical suffering, it was also awful to watch a loved one suffer emotionally.

Karries let me know that all the money to cover the funeral did come in, from the pockets of generous strangers, and even covered some outstanding bills from Renee's cancer treatment. It became clear that my job was definitely the headstone.

After a bit of research, I found a great monument company I really liked called Pyramid Memorials. My contact there was familiar with the Finneys' story from the news. She scheduled a meeting with Karries and her siblings, and arranged for me to join them via conference call. It would be the first time I would speak on the phone with Karries's siblings.

After introductions were made on the call, David kicked off the conversation by announcing, "Well, I brought my drawing."

There was a bit of dead air on the phone before I heard Karries say, "What are you talking about?"

David answered, "I drew some pictures of what I want on the headstone."

Though I couldn't see their faces, I imagined how surprised Karries and Davion would be in that moment.

David had drawn a flowery vine with some butterflies. His sisters received his ideas and agreed that the image he'd drawn would be perfect for their mother's headstone. And, of course, it was about so much more than the drawing. His contribution allowed his sisters to see that he had been processing his grief in his own way. Though it would still be a process, both were relieved. As I often did, I felt honored to be invited to participate in such a sacred family moment.

Framed by David's artwork, Renee's tombstone read:

A Mother, Grandmother, Daughter, Sister
& Aunt Who's Forever in Our Hearts.
Forever Remembered and Forever Missed

And at the bottom, in a much smaller font:

He Knows Your Name

CALIFORNIA

As the late summer months wore on, my dad's health began to fail. I realized that I would soon be sitting where these three brave young people were sitting. My father died August 11 and just two weeks later Pyramid Memorials called to let me know that Renee's headstone had been placed.

Since May I'd known that I wanted to be present to dedicate this headstone, and now the timing was absurd. I'd buried my dad and taken Caroline to college, and Steve was about to leave for Ukraine. I was tired emotionally and physically.

As Steve and I looked into booking the flights and hotel, we realized it was Labor Day weekend and that making plans was going to be difficult. Miraculously, the flights worked out and Steve found me a beachside hotel in Carlsbad located right between my daughter Lauren, who lived near Los Angeles, and my brother-in-law, who was also in Southern California.

The day I left Indianapolis, emotionally weary, I wondered why on earth I was traveling to the West Coast. The timing was awful. I was depleted. When I left the airport in a rental car, I was still unsure. When I pulled up to the hotel, though, I was captured by the beauty: the hotel was right on the ocean, on a cliff that overlooked the beach. From the moment I stepped outside, I felt as if it was healing me, moment by moment. I considered it the biggest gift from God. I could not have planned anything better than being outside walking the shoreline, and enjoying time with my precious daughter and her husband. It was amazing.

Saturday morning, on the day of the ceremony, I met Karries, Davion, and David. It was a sweet service and I loved being with Renee's precious, loving children and their extended family. Renee's mother was a delicate little lady. Because she was blind, Davion had guided her to the plot. That I was allowed to be present was a gift I'll never forget.

When I flew home on Tuesday morning, September 2, I assumed that my part in the Finneys' story was over.

The Finneys, however, weren't through being grateful.

A THANK YOU

In January, I received a phone call from a number I didn't recognize. It had been a very full day because I'd spoken at the Indiana State House to give testimony for the Baby Box initiative before the House of Representatives. I'd been invited to speak by a firefighter who had been actively advocating for the Safe Haven Baby Box law to be passed in Indiana. I wanted to do my part to ensure that no other baby was disposed of the way that Baby Moses had been. The call came just as I was stepping back into my home. I recognized a Chicago area code.

It was a producer from the *Steve Harvey* show. "The Finney family nominated you as a thank you for what you did for them," she explained. "We'd like to bring you to the *Steve Harvey* show as a thank you."

I didn't know what to think. I didn't need to be thanked, but of course wanted to honor the Finneys' kind gesture.

I asked, "Are the kids going to be there? That is going to make a better show."

"No," she answered. "The kids won't be there. It is about you guys and what you did, and us thanking you for being a Good Samaritan."

Convinced that sharing these stories was the way they multiplied, as others had the opportunity to hear them, I was happy to be on board. I agreed to show up at the show's Chicago studio the following week.

The next day, though, I received a call back from the producer. Storms in the east meant that their regularly scheduled guests were unable to get in to Chicago. They'd arranged for Yvette to fly from California and wanted to film the following day, if I'd be able to make it. The next morning I was on my way to Chicago.

A SURPRISE FROM STEVE

Seated beside her in the show's "green room," I loved meeting Yvette and hearing her describe how the whole story had begun. She'd had the privilege of attending Renee's funeral and told me how lovely it had been to meet the Finneys. While we were backstage, assistant producers had prepped us for the questions Steve Harvey would ask us and we practiced how we would respond. In the final few moments before we were brought onstage, we each took a few deep breaths to calm our nerves!

When the taping began, Steve gave each of us the opportunity to answer a brief question and then affirmed, "I think that you are two really very generous women. I just thought that the story was so heartwarming when I heard it."

Then the story took an unexpected turn when he added, "But I gotta be a little honest with you: I didn't bring you here just for you to tell your story."

What was happening? This felt like the moment when the talk show host would tell a guest they were getting some exciting surprise gift. But Yvette and I didn't need anything. The kids did.

Steve continued, "I've got some folks here who want to thank you."

As the studio audience began clapping, Karries, Davion, and David walked onstage. They looked beautiful. The girls were dressed up, and the show's stylists had dolled them up with stunning hair and makeup. They looked gorgeous. Sweet David looked so handsome wearing a sharp blue sweater and tailored dress slacks. We all hugged each other, crying.

Then Yvette just squeaked out the words, "Hi, guys."

Steve gave Davion the opportunity to thank us first.

She began, "I want to thank you guys from the bottom of my heart. You guys are blessings not just to me but to my family, and we love you guys so much."

Catching her breath, Yvette said, "We love you too."

Davion continued, "You guys were complete strangers that helped us, but now you guys are not strangers anymore, you are *family* to us and I want to thank you."

More clapping. More hugging. Then David, nervous but brave, thanked us for helping them have a proper burial for their mom. His face, so different than the sullen teen his big sisters had been so worried about, was beaming.

Then Karries, the new matriarch, explained, with tears in her eyes, how difficult it was to wake up and not have the resources to bury your mother. "And then to wake up the next day with no worries, is . . . indescribable. And I can't thank you guys enough." She also added, "The best thing I can do is just live my life the best way I can and just pay it forward, just keep paying it forward and change someone's life like you changed ours. I love you guys so much."

More tears. More hugs. More clapping.

But that wasn't all.

A GIFT FOR DAVID

As cameras rolled, Steve Harvey said to David, "I want you in my mentoring camp."

In various cities across America, the Steve Harvey Mentoring Camp is introducing young men who live in households headed by single women to role models who provide positive examples of manhood. It's a four-day program designed to prepare teens for a future where they are strong, responsible, and productive men. When Steve offered this opportunity to David, Karries started crying hysterically. "This is what I wanted. I wanted this for David so bad," she said.

The segment that aired on national television ended with Steve Harvey giving Karries a five-thousand-dollar prepaid Visa gift card from one of the show's sponsors, to help during the difficult time.

FRUITFULNESS

After the show—the first national media exposure for He Knows Your Name—my in-box was slammed with all kinds of requests.

"I have experienced so much loss and now I am going to get married to my high school sweetheart. Can you pay for my wedding?"

"We've had so much loss and now my son is back in school. He has $7000 in student loans. Can you help?"

"I saw you on *Steve Harvey*. I am 88 years old and my neighbors take care of me. It is their anniversary. I want to buy them a TV from HH Gregg. It is only $250. Will you buy it?"

Requests poured in.

Donations trickled in.

Requests I'd expected, but the donations were a happy surprise.

EXPOSURE

Whenever I've had the opportunity for media exposure, I have prayed that the stories of God's redemption would trigger others to respond to the still small voice of God wooing each one of us to follow him. I'm never looking to generate more work for myself! My heart soars, though, when the Spirit lubricates the story in such a way that something "clicks" for someone else. One woman at church lets me know that she had the opportunity to pray with a friend who'd been grieving a child lost to abortion for decades. A military police officer, passionate to see fewer babies abandoned, lobbies for more effective measures. Someone else at last understands the magnitude of a loss that a loved one has endured and reaches out to say, "Now I see. I know. I care."

I am so grateful that my friend first emailed me the news story about the Finneys. Such an absurdly unlikely series of circumstances that finally connected me to those three children *must* have been divinely inspired. But if there comes a day when so many Christians begin to recognize and respond to God's constant whisper, "Come here, daughter.

Come here, son. Let's do this together," I will be delighted to sit back—between assignments!—and prayerfully cheer them on.

By God's grace, may it one day be so.

When I first heard about the Finney children, it was because they were financially unable to provide a dignified burial for the mother they loved. When the bulk of their financial needs were met, by the gracious outpouring of love from the community, I might have stepped away. But God was showing me that his work through me was about more than writing a check or networking to orchestrate arrangements. Graciously, he allowed me to remind Karries, Davion, and David—with my spiritual, emotional, and physical presence—that God saw their suffering and cared deeply for each one of them.

CHAPTER 11

Twenty-Four Mug Shots

When I heard that fifteen-year-old Dominique Allen had gone missing from a sleepover with friends, I thought of all the sleepovers my own teenage girls had been a part of over the years. And by sleepover, of course, I mean *not* sleeping. I mean laughing and talking about boys and snacking and arguing and listening to music and watching movies. That's what Dominique Allen had been doing when she went missing on a Saturday night late in August.

Dominique had been at the home of one of her sisters, thirty-year-old Mareeka, with several other girls. In the early morning hours of August 31, she stepped onto Mareeka's porch to cool off after a disagreement with one of those friends. When the other girls went back inside, Dominique continued to stew on the porch. She was last seen around 4:30 a.m.

When her sister woke a few hours later, she realized Dominique was gone. When Dominique didn't answer her cell phone, Mareeka inquired with her friends. They hadn't seen her since the argument. Mareeka called her father to see if Dominique had returned home. She checked in with family members to see if Dominique had shown up, but no one had seen her. Growing worried, Mareeka called the police department to file a missing persons report.

About the same time Mareeka was explaining what she knew of Dominique's absence, a man walking his dog about a mile from Mareeka's home discovered the body of a young woman who'd been strangled and asphyxiated. A plastic bag was over her head and the bottom half of her body had been burned. When police investigating the discovery realized the body matched the description of the missing girl, they alerted Dominique's family. On Tuesday, two days after she'd gone missing, her body was positively identified.

What happened during the eight hours between Dominique's disappearance and the discovery of her body wasn't clear.

The pieces of the puzzle just didn't add up. Investigators noted that Dominique's phone was still inside her sister's house, suggesting she may not have left voluntarily. Her family says she would never have gotten into a car with a stranger. They knew of no one who'd want to harm the vivacious teen.

Investigators later discovered Dominique's purse and sandals at an abandoned house, about a block from where her body was found. Charred grass in the yard where her body was found indicated that she'd been set on fire there. Marion County Coroners would later reveal that, graciously, the absence of smoke in her lungs suggests she hadn't been alive when her body was set ablaze.

The investigation into Dominique's murder dragged on for weeks. Pursuing hundreds of tips, police would think they were close to a suspect and the lead would turn out to be a dead end. Dominique's family offered a three-thousand-dollar reward for information leading to the capture of her killer.

Almost three weeks after Dominique's attack and murder, on Friday, September 19, her family held a rally and vigil in downtown Indianapolis. The flyer inviting the public announced, "We won't stop until justice is served." At 5:00 p.m. the rally speakers, featuring a host of pastors and leaders in the community, as well as a group called The Concerned Clergy of Indianapolis, encouraged the public to come forward with any information that might help detectives solve the case.

The next day was Dominique's funeral. The unsolved case was upsetting not just to the Allen family but to the whole community. They were undone that there was not yet a single suspect in the case. The lead detective working the case was also frustrated. He'd even solicited advice from several retired Indianapolis Metropolitan Police Department detectives. While nothing would have made the day of Dominique's funeral bearable, the fact that her killer was still free and on the loose tormented her family.

Except that her killer wasn't as free as they thought.

ONGOING INVESTIGATION

The day Dominique was killed, August 31, school had already begun in Indianapolis and the kids were out for the long Labor Day weekend. As Dominique's murder hit the local news, I was in California with Renee Finney's children.

I didn't learn about it until the Monday after I returned home. Jessica, one of the women in the Monday Bible study that has met in my home for fifteen years, asked our group to pray for Dominique's family, friends, and community. This was one of those holy "referrals" where the person reporting a need steps with God into the lives of those who are suffering. Jessica ministers to some high school girls at Dominique's high school in her role as a youth group volunteer at Connection Pointe Christian Church. Many of the girls she knew there were distraught. After our Bible study met and prayed for the situation, Jessica sent me a link to the horrific story.

When I reached out to Dominique's sister, Mareeka, I learned that plans for Dominique's funeral were already in motion. In that respect, it felt a bit like the Finney family's situation. When I'm with a family at the front end of their tragedy, I know that their immediate need is often burial. Their lives have been turned upside down and they're just going through the motions, trying to put one foot in front of the other. Typically, the last thing in the world they're thinking about is a headstone.

When Mareeka and I spoke on the phone, I asked, "What do you need? What are your immediate concerns?"

Without hesitation she answered, "We need a headstone."

Her answer took me off guard. And it's why I knew, in an instant, that

God was orchestrating the connection. And though I had no idea what was on the other side of this door, it was clear that God was inviting me to step through it.

I'd pored over the news coverage and I was still curious about several things.

"When I read the news," I probed gently, "I see your name and your dad's name, but I don't see anything about a mom."

Mareeka's answer broke my heart.

"My mom died two years ago. She died of Crohn's disease and doesn't have a headstone. We're going to bury them together."

As she spoke I imagined my own mother's headstone where I was able to visit, weep, grieve.

Mareeka continued to explain how, although her mom wasn't buried in a double plot, they were hoping for a headstone—displaying both names—that would include a cremation container under it for Dominique's ashes. It's why they'd chosen cremation.

Suddenly the reason for Mareeka's awareness became clear: she knew they needed a headstone because, for two years, they'd not had one for their mother.

When Mareeka and I spoke, the family was planning to hold Dominique's funeral with her body, and then have her cremated. As Mareeka shared, it was clear that I was in over my head. I didn't have a relationship yet with the funeral home they'd chosen and had only a peripheral connection to the cemetery where their mom, Sherri Allen, had been buried. And the business of burying an extra person in a single plot was new as well. Because I didn't know if I'd be able to secure the resources to help it happen, I was very cautious with my language, explaining that I'd need to make some phone calls to see what was available.

As I got in touch with my contacts who I thought might help, person after person directed me to Thomas Monument. Sure enough, they had some ideas. I called Mareeka back and we made an appointment to meet at Thomas Monument. She said her brother would join her. When we met there in late September, after speaking on the phone so many times, we hugged and I told Mareeka how nice it was to meet.

With a sweet smile she replied, "Our voices are already best friends."

As Mareeka and her brother Michael weighed choices for the headstone, I was delighted to learn more about Dominique—to glimpse the human side of her that her attacker never saw, that folks who watched the news never got to see.

Dominique had served in her school's anti-bullying organization.

Her favorite color was red.

She loved fashion and wanted to be a model.

The ninth grader hoped to attend Spelman College in Atlanta.

She loved to take selfies and post them on social media.

A tiara had rested on Dominique's casket at the funeral service.

She and her mother had both loved roses.

As I was privileged to know just a bit of this young woman and her journey, I was reminded of the One who knew her name. Who was intimately acquainted with every moment of her life. Who was with her until the end. And beyond.

Through Mareeka's and Michael's love for their sister, God had brought Dominique to life in my heart and mind. As if I'd actually known her, I came to love her the way I love my daughters' girlfriends and my girlfriends' daughters. Knowing Dominique in that way, knowing Mareeka and Michael, truly felt like a holy privilege.

Of course "privilege" had begun to take on a whole new meaning! In relationship after relationship, I began to see how my privileges—education, comfort, wealth, social status—had actually been a barrier to connecting with so many of the ones God loved who had access to fewer resources. By no intention of my own, they had kept me from knowing teenagers like Dominique and Tim Bray. They had kept me from engaging with the moms of joyful little ones like Donasty and Annaliese. My "privileges" had kept me from enjoying the affection of three generations of the Laudig family.

Through Holy Spirit nudgings and my yeses, these privileges that could so easily be used to build walls were being used by God to construct bridges. Forging relationships with these beloved ones, whom I would never have had access to know without these privileges, smacked of the upside-down kingdom Jesus had described: "Whoever finds their life will lose it, and whoever loses their life for my sake will find it" (Matthew 10:39).

Compared to those who have literally lost their lives for Christ, it's fair to say I've lost little—time, money, sleep. But with every tentative yes when God opened a new door, I gained everything.

KEEPING VIGIL

Dominique's story hit the national news related to a string of unsolved cases involving slain teens.

Her family and community continued to organize walks and vigils to keep awareness high. They canvassed the high school, talking to students in hopes of discovering a clue that might unlock the mystery of her death. They asked to see students' phones, searching for any shred of evidence that might help detectives—such as a text that may have been sent that evening. They had rallies in parking lots. The Concerned Clergy group continued to support Dominique's family. They believed that somebody had to know something or have seen something.

I attended one rally in Haughville, the neighborhood where Dominique's body had been found. It's a rough area of our city. We met in the parking lot of an elementary school there to continue to raise awareness about Dominique's case. It had been almost three months and the police still had no suspects. Dominique's family and the community were growing increasingly frustrated.

That morning Mareeka introduced me to two African-American men involved with Concerned Clergy. Reverend Day and Elder Rush wore black trench coats and black hats. They have a strong presence in the community and are well respected throughout the city for their efforts to bring faith and peace to the community. Their organization is concerned with quality education, economics, housing, health care, and legislation within the city. They're advocates for those who, too often, aren't heard by those in power. I knew they would be standing with this family until justice was served.

A few days after the rally, as Mareeka and I discussed the headstone dedication, it occurred to me that this would be yet a different kind of headstone dedication. Although the funeral had already taken place, it would also be Dominique's *burial*. Her remains were still legally in the care of the funeral home director, who would keep them until they were released to a family member, who would deliver them to the monument company. When the cemetery received the monument containing Dominique's ashes, it would be set immediately.

This would already be a complicated conversation between a number of parties, but a wish of Mareeka's made it a bit more unwieldy. Mareeka had ordered six necklaces, for herself and family members, with cylinders to hold Dominique's ashes. The pendant hanging from each chain was heart shaped, with a metal cylinder inside to hold the ashes. The six cylinders would go to Mareeka, her father, two sisters, and Dominique's nieces. One niece, Mareeka's daughter, was Dominique's age and had been very close to her.

When we received the call that the headstone had been completed, Mareeka and I planned the dedication of the headstone for November 17. But when Mareeka was called in to work that day, we looked at her schedule and postponed it until November 29.

CLOSE TO THE HEART

On November 20, Mareeka called me from work to say that the necklaces had arrived. I picked them up from her, along with the ashes that had been reserved and given to the family, and took them to the monument company where the ashes would be put into the necklaces.

When I looked over the necklaces, though, the first clasp I tried to open broke right in my hand. Inspecting the others, I noticed that all the clasps seemed flimsy. On the way back to meet Mareeka when she got off work, I stopped by a silver store at the mall, testing lobster claw chains to make sure they had a sturdy spring mechanism. I picked out sturdy chains for each of the heart pendants.

Mareeka's kind gift to her family, glass pendants to keep Dominique close to their hearts, wasn't so different from what I, and others, hoped to do through He Knows Your Name. One temptation in grief can be to protect one's self by not facing the loss that's been endured. Wanting to avoid pain, either consciously or unconsciously, those who've endured a life-altering loss may move *past* a loss without moving *through* it. They welcome a speedy return to everyday rhythms of work, church, or school. They may numb themselves with food, busyness, entertainment, or substances to avoid feeling pain. They might even avoid thinking about or talking about the person who's been lost. And while the shortcut might spare these mourners pain in the short run, it also robs them of the opportunity to face their loss squarely, grieve well, and become available to God's healing touch. Just as I believe that a headstone can help to facilitate God's healing process in human hearts, I could also imagine that these necklaces might do the same. As I drove to meet Mareeka, I prayed that they might.

I could see the excitement on Mareeka's face when I walked in with the pendants. Her shift had just ended. I asked her to sit down on a stool at the counter so I could clip one on her neck. She was beaming.

Glancing down at the pendant, she promised, "I'm never going to take this off."

"You can't say that," I reminded her. "You don't want to wear this in the shower!"

Mareeka and I chatted a bit about who would receive the other chains and then, as I prepared to leave, precious Mareeka became quiet.

"Come outside with me," she instructed. "I want to tell you something."

When we stepped outside, clear of the doorway, she revealed, "They have a suspect, but they're not announcing it until Friday."

It was the best news she could have shared.

"Nobody knows," she continued in a low voice, "but I know that I can trust you. I am so relieved."

Without words, I hugged her as we celebrated together.

That was Wednesday.

A SUSPECT

The next day my phone started blowing up with calls from the media, who knew about the suspect.

I immediately texted Mareeka about it, assuring her, "I didn't tell anyone!"

She knew that.

Apparently the police department begins to posture itself when they know an arrest is imminent. When they announced that there would be a press conference Friday morning at 9:00 a.m., the media put the pieces together. Mareeka and I both agreed not to talk to the media about the case.

At the press conference, police revealed that a man named William Gholston Senior had been arrested for the abduction, rape, and murder of Dominique Allen, saying that DNA evidence had been key in identifying the suspect.

A few days earlier William Gholston had been stopped in northern Indiana for a traffic violation. When the arresting officer checked his identity, he discovered that Mr. Gholston, who had a long criminal record, had violated parole by leaving Marion County. So he was brought back to be jailed in Marion County.

His arrest had nothing to do with Dominique Allen.

But when DNA evidence recovered from Dominique's body was run through a criminal database and discovered to match Gholston's, he was, quite conveniently, already locked up in the Marion County Jail.

That week two images in the *Indianapolis Star* caught my attention. One was a string of twenty-four mug shots of William Gholston Senior, lined up like postage stamps. The other—snapped at the press conference event—was of Dominique's father, Louis Allen, exuberant, hugging his oldest daughter, Shenika.

CLOSURE AT LAST

Fortuitously, the new headstone dedication date turned out to be one week after the press conference announcing Gholston's arrest. The sense of closure was an incredible blessing to the family who, along with the Indiana Metro Police Department, had worked so hard to identify Dominique's killer so that she could, at last, rest in peace.

After giving it much consideration, Dominique's family decided to welcome the media to her headstone dedication. Mareeka explained to me over the phone, "We are so thankful to the community who has walked through this with us. We don't know how we would have gotten through this without community support. We want Reverend Day and Elder Rush there. We want the media there, but we have some concerns."

Several other memorials to Dominique had been erected in other parts of the city—at the high school she had attended and at the site where her body had been found—and those had both been vandalized. Mareeka said her family was concerned that, if the location got out, the headstone would be vandalized also. I shared their concern.

How could we invite the media and keep the location of Dominique's remains a secret?

In the end, Mareeka and I decided to divide and conquer. Because the event was by invitation only, she would be responsible for alerting and educating the family and friends who'd been invited and I'd take responsibility for the media, policemen, and cemetery staff. We would allow the media to report that the event happened, and even show the people who attended, but they couldn't show *any* headstone with a name on it. They couldn't show the gate, the name of the cemetery, or the houses lining the cemetery.

It was, though, even more unwieldy than that. Anyone attending might snap a photograph with a phone that has a location device and then share that picture, sending along the location where the photo was taken. So I was diligent to contact every officer, every media contact, and every person who worked at the cemetery, securing their word to keep the location secret and writing down the name of each person I spoke to.

FOLDING CHAIRS

For three months, Dominique's family had *stood up* for justice. And as I prayed about the service, Jesus gave me a very clear picture that I had to have chairs so that I could invite the family to *sit*.

Yet on the morning of the service, as Dominique's family and my family began to arrive, I could see that the cemetery had not put the chairs out. Steve asked if I wanted him to run to the cemetery office to find chairs. Though I appreciated the offer, I didn't want us to be frantic about it. I'd come to rely on God's steadfast presence, especially when I was juggling so many moving parts.

So we waited.

At eleven, when the service was scheduled to begin, we were still waiting on Dominique's brother to arrive. At that moment a rickety old brown car pulled up, and out stepped a man in a worn green work jumpsuit. Moseying around to the trunk, in no rush at all, he opened it up and began pulling out rickety old folding chairs. Steve and a few others helped him unload and set up the chairs in the soggy grass. I directed them to create a semicircle near the headstone.

Then I looked at Mareeka and her family and shared what had been on my heart.

"For three months I've watched you, as a family, stand," I began. "I've seen you stand in vigilance, advocating for justice; stand next to each other as pillars of strength; stand and march to bring awareness; stand in hope that an answer would come; stand and trust as a team of criminal justice professionals fought for you; and stand in truth as you held out hope that your prayers would be answered."

As I glanced from face to face, I saw faithful warriors who had earned their rest.

"Today," I offered, "I invite you to sit down."

They all sat down.

"It is time for you to sit down and rest. Your work is done. Today is a day of relief and closure. I invite you to sit down physically, emotionally, mentally, and be at peace and rest."

The rest of us stood.

As I moved through the service I'd prepared, I noticed Elder Rush holding a book open. That little glimpse, and a nudge of God's Spirit, signaled to me that I needed to invite him to participate. *How, Lord?*

When it was time to recite the Lord's Prayer, I asked him if he'd lead us. In a deep, beautiful voice he did. As he prayed, I stepped closer to peek at the book he was holding. It was a minister's funeral guide. I noticed the word "committal."

At the point in the service when a prayer of committal was appropriate, I whispered, "Would you like to do this?"

I wanted to honor him, but didn't want to put him on the spot.

He answered, "I told Louis I'd do the committal for her burial."

I hadn't known what was spoken between Elder Rush and Dominique's father, and so his acceptance confirmed the nudge God had given me.

Standing in front of the headstone, with Reverend Day at his side, Elder Rush opened his black leather volume and offered a prayer of committal, entrusting Dominique's body to the Lord. Then, to my surprise, he expressed their gratitude for the ministry of He Knows Your Name, acknowledging that this family had been well served. In an absurd situation in which a middle-aged, blond, white woman stood out in the crowd, it was a generous gesture I'd not expected. Though I did stand out, Elder Rush had so kindly communicated that I still *belonged*.

I wasn't naive. I understood how it looked. Over several years, folks in Indianapolis could read an article in the paper about a headstone dedication and see, in the accompanying photo, only a rich white lady from North Indianapolis who could afford to purchase a headstone. Skeptics might believe me to be a religious nut or a do-gooder looking for a publicity op. Others—those who actually attended the services or the ones who sat in the folding chairs—had been able to discern a deeper authenticity in the ways God had knit together the hearts of wildly different people. And I believe, at Dominique's service and across the spectrum of He Knows Your Name's ministry, there was even a deeper layer of spiritual reality unfolding: God longs for reconciliation between once-separated people, and that was being realized.

I still don't understand entirely why the great privilege is mine.

My gut and my experience, though, tell me that experiencing the reality of the kingdom Jesus ushered in is available to any fool for Christ who is willing to say yes when God calls.

THE LONG HAUL

The service concluded, and as we walked back toward our vehicles, Shenika walked beside me. She was quiet for several moments and then, with a serious tone, posed a question to me.

"So," she queried, "are you going the distance with us or were you just doing this?"

Her question caught me off guard.

I think what she was really asking was, "Are you really our friend? Do you really care?" The trial for William Gholston was approaching and she wanted to know if I'd continue to journey with them. I'd seen on the news that the family had vowed to be present at every single one of William Gholston Senior's legal proceedings.

What flashed into my mind in that moment was my stint on jury duty, three years prior, in a double homicide. *Do I really have it in me to support this family in this kind of way?*

I answered carefully. Honestly.

"I will track with you emotionally," I offered, "but sitting through the trial is not something I can do on a daily basis. I will be there when I can."

Nodding, Shenika accepted what I was able to offer.

When Mareeka contacted me three months later to let me know about a pretrial hearing, it was my pleasure to join them in the courtroom at the City County building.

William Gholston was eventually tried, eighteen months after Dominique's murder. During jury selection I sat in the courtroom praying for each person who was interviewed. The same afternoon, before Mareeka testified, we slipped away to pray together. As we held one another's hands, I noticed the silver bracelet I'd chosen to wear that morning, one with charms reading *comfort, faith, hope,* and *peace.* I unlatched it and slipped it onto Mareeka's wrist as a kind of spiritual armor to gird her for what she was about to do. Strengthened by God's grace, she was brave and confident as she testified.

The swift trial lasted only two and a half days. After the prosecution played a video of an interview with Gholston where he learned that his DNA had been recovered from the crime scene, the defense rested. The jury deliberated less than three hours before pronouncing their unanimous verdict: *guilty.* When William Gholston was finally sentenced, not only did he receive sixty-four years in prison but the judge added a "habitual offender" qualifier which added twenty years to that sentence. In addition to the horrific killing of Dominique Allen, Gholston's previous crimes represented by those twenty-four mug shots had been acknowledged in the judgment. The evening news showing the Allen family rejoicing on the courthouse steps was a beautiful glimpse of those who'd been set free when justice was done, allowing the Allens finally to rest and to focus on creating a lasting legacy for precious Dominique.

At every juncture of a difficult journey, including this one, there are opportunities to leave the journey. The temptation is always to distance one's self from pain. To move away from those who suffer. To protect one's self. To avoid the agony of others that elicits our own pain. Dodging discomfort, we comfort ourselves with whatever soothes our deep ache. Spiritual writer and theologian Henri Nouwen identifies this temptation. In his book *The Inner Voice of Love*, he exhorts,

> You can look at your life as a large cone that becomes narrower the deeper you go. There are many doors in that cone that give you chances to leave the journey. But you have been closing these doors one after the other, making yourself go deeper and deeper into your center. You know that Jesus is waiting for you at the end, just as you know that he is guiding you as you move in that direction. Every time you close another door—be it the door of immediate satisfaction, the door of distracting entertainment, the door of busyness, the door of guilt and worry, or the door of self-rejection—you commit yourself to go deeper into your heart and thus deeper into the heart of God.[9]

This is the path that God invites each one of us to sojourn, growing closer and closer to his heart.

For most of us, it won't involve harrowing criminality, eager media, or courtroom drama. But choosing to follow Jesus into the places he goes will mean choosing to move into places of pain. Calling a friend who's separated from her husband. Writing a note to a young woman after her fifth miscarriage. Taking a neighbor to lunch after her father dies. Visiting a church member after she's received a terrifying diagnosis. As we join others in their suffering, we imitate the One who entered into death itself out of love for you and for me.

People who've heard about He Knows Your Name sometimes marvel at the kinds of situations I have ended up in after saying yes to God. They mistakenly think I'm some other breed of creature who is braver or stronger or full of more faith than the average Christian.

I'm not.

I am, however, convinced that as we move deeper into the tight spaces, those places of pain and loss and discomfort, we find Jesus there.

By the time I met the Allen family I had a broad understanding that the mission of He Knows Your Name was to honor children and their families by offering dignity in death. But as I walked with the Allen family, as I stood beside Reverend Day and Elder Rush to honor Dominique and her family, I sensed that God had been quietly orchestrating something even deeper. God was allowing his body—too long fractured by racial and social divides—to minister side by side to the world God loves. Though it was not something I ever could have planned, I thanked God for the holy privilege of being a part of it.

CHAPTER 12

The Small Flying Defender

When Nicholas's body had been found, I had to wait thirteen long months to bury him. Fifteen more months would pass before Dixie's and George's headstones would be set. But, like labor pains, the invitations from God had been coming closer together. Just one month after the dedication of Dominique's headstone, a hiker at Eagle Creek Park found a newborn baby girl wrapped inside a sweatshirt just thirty yards from a parking area. The blue sweatshirt read, "Aviation Maintenance, Vincennes University, Indianapolis." Shaken, the woman called the police who pronounced the baby dead at the scene.

Two days later Alfie issued a statement that it was, at that time, unknown if the infant had been delivered dead or alive, as its gestational age had yet to be determined. Homicide detectives believe the infant, who may have been as little as one day old, was born at the park. The umbilical cord and placenta were still attached.

The infant girl had a large amount of dark hair and appeared to be Caucasian. Her body revealed pressure points from where she'd lain on the ground. The right side of her face had deformities, and her left and right arms also appeared deformed. Whether these were birth defects or were suffered after birth was unclear. Tire tracks were found nearby.

FLYING DEFENDER

When I called Alfie, she told me that the coroner technician for the baby found in the woods was Jessica Miller, who was being supervised by Amanda, the young woman who'd cared for Baby Moses.

After speaking with Alfie, I called Jessica to let her know I was interested in caring for the baby's body. Though I knew there were no guarantees, something in my heart—perhaps informed by my experience with Moses—told me that this baby would eventually be released to me.

Though Indiana's Safe Haven law had been passed to protect infants like this one from being abandoned by desperate parents, this little one had not been protected. Several news outlets had reported that this babe had been found just two miles from a fire station, where she might have been safely relinquished without legal consequence. As I searched for more information online about the baby girl, I saw a photo of the blue sweatshirt in which she'd been wrapped. Police were appealing to anyone who recognized the sweatshirt to come forward with any information that might be useful. Though dozens, possibly hundreds, had been sold at the school's bookstore throughout the years, investigators hoped to elicit some useful nugget of information from concerned viewers. When I saw "aviation," as well as the proud wings on the insignia, designed like the honorary plastic ones children were once given on airplanes, a long-forgotten memory flooded my mind.

When each of my children was in fifth grade, they were assigned to portray a famous person from history and embody their character in what amounted to a living wax museum. One little girl offered a stunning and memorable performance as Amelia Earhart. So when I saw the "aviation" sweatshirt and this memory hit me, I just knew that this little baby girl was to be named "Amelia."

I shared the name with my family and continued to hold it close to my heart.

WHAT'S IN A NAME

When I researched the meaning of *Amelia*, I found it meant "defender." It was easy to imagine that this precious little one might indeed become a defender of the state's Safe Haven law so that the law might be more effective for other vulnerable infants.

Two days after the news broke, my Anna, who'd been following the story of the baby found in the woods, texted me simply, "Middle?"

She was asking if I'd chosen a middle name for Amelia. I hadn't considered it until Anna asked, but I suddenly knew who I wanted to choose it. Jessica had been working so intimately with Amelia, and my recent meeting with her supervisor, Amanda, had reminded me of how much care and emotional energy these servants pour out for each child with whom they work.

When I called Jessica to extend the invitation, she agreed, but said she'd like to take a few days to decide. We spoke again a few days later when I called her for any updates on the case.

"So," I asked, "did you decide on a middle name for Amelia?"

"Well . . ." Jessica hedged. "I'm not religious like you are."

I chuckled, amused by the disclaimer, wondering what was coming next.

"So, what did you choose?" I asked.

"Grace," Jessica announced.

"Hmm . . . ," I said, absorbing the name. I was curious.

"And what does that mean to you?" I pressed.

Jessica explained, "It means she wasn't alone and that God was with her."

Jessica's insight reminded me that *not-religious* people can often be the best kind.

I told her I thought it was perfect.

Though I had no idea how long the criminal investigation would take, I knew to be patient. After Amelia had been with the coroner's office for just one week though, I was told I should call Alfie in four days.

My curiosity bubbled during the wait.

When my phone rang two days before my scheduled call to Alfie, I recognized her number. She told me to begin lining up my ducks for a Friday or Monday release of the body. Surprised, but trusting Alfie's experience and sense of timing, I began orchestrating details with the funeral home and cemetery. When Alfie called me back on Friday, I assumed she was calling to let me know Amelia's paperwork had been completed and she could be released to me.

But that's not why Alfie had called.

"Linda," she said solemnly, "I have another baby."

A one-year-old named Harmoni had been flown to Riley's Hospital from her home in eastern Illinois.

Alfie continued, "This baby's mother is currently incarcerated in Ohio."

BABY HARMONI

Several weeks earlier, a prison social worker had delivered the news to an inmate I'll call "Geraldine Green" that, while she'd been behind bars, her baby daughter had died. The circumstances around that death that I read in the coroner's report Alfie faxed over after we spoke were terribly unnerving.

Geraldine Green had been imprisoned after standing trial for manipulating two of her older children, ages six and eight, to steal more than $100,000 worth of jewelry while she distracted the store clerk. She'd been pregnant during the crime, so Harmoni had been born in the county jail. Since birth, Harmoni had been in the care of others. First she was in the custody of a friend of Geraldine's who lived in Atlanta. When this woman's home burned down, Harmoni's care was transferred to a woman named Tyshema Young, identified in the police report only as a distant relative.

Four children lived in a home with Tyshema and her boyfriend. I assume they were hers, though their identities weren't specified. In addition to one-year-old Harmoni, the other children were two, four, and five years old. The police report states that when the children awoke on the morning of December 5, 2014, the two-year-old wanted to take a bath and ran the bath water. The two-year-old and five-year-old got into the bathtub while Tyshema slept in a bedroom and her boyfriend slept on the couch. At some point, Harmoni climbed up on the ledge of the bathtub and fell in. The report says that when the four-year-old child entered the bathroom, and saw Harmoni floating, she awakened Tyshema's boyfriend and announced, "Harmoni's dead."

Racing to the bathroom, he pulled her from the water, called 911, and began CPR. Emergency medics arrived shortly after, took over CPR, and transported Harmoni to Heartland Regional Medical Center in Marion, Illinois. When she could be stabilized, she was flown to Riley Hospital in Indianapolis to receive critical care. Unfortunately, her prognosis was poor. Harmoni Jackson was pronounced dead at 2:05 p.m., December 5, 2014.

Because I'd seen how the mother of "Baby Doe"—aka Nichole—had been vilified in the media, I tried to reserve judgment. After all, I remembered what it was like to care for four young children. Was it possible that the same thing might have happened just as easily to me or someone I knew? Had it simply been an unavoidable tragedy, or was there anything that might have been done differently? My mind raced.

The circumstances seemed so absurd that I scoured the coroner's report to learn more.

According to a representative from Child Protective Services in Marion, Illinois, just four months earlier Harmoni had endured a near-drowning incident. Tyshema's boyfriend reported at the time that he'd been giving Harmoni a bath and that she'd been sitting in a tub safety ring suctioned to the bottom of the bathtub. The boyfriend claimed that at some point the suction cups must have come loose because he found Harmoni tipped over in the bathtub and underwater.

To my ear, that story sounded fishy.

He "found" Harmoni underwater? I *had* juggled baths for four children and knew how quickly things could get chaotic. Any mother of *one* would agree. But where had he gone that he would return to "find" her underwater?

My heart ached.

In the wake of that first incident, Harmoni had been transported to an area hospital and was kept under observation for twenty-three hours. She was never taken to a doctor for a follow-up. In fact, with the exception of the daylong hospitalization, she'd never once visited a doctor in her short lifetime.

Feeling nauseous, I laid the report down on my desk.

CAN YOU DOUBLE YOUR EFFORTS?

Because Alfie and I already had an appointment to sign papers for Amelia on Monday, January 12, and I'd arranged transport of Amelia's body to the funeral home the following morning, I had to ask the question which had burst into my mind.

"Could Harmoni be ready to be released on Monday? Can the paperwork be ready when I come Monday morning for Amelia?"

Alfie said it could be done.

I called Geraldine Green's prison social worker to secure the release of Harmoni's body. They agreed to sign the paperwork the coroner needed to release the body to me. When it had been faxed over, the coroner's office would forward a copy to me.

As soon as we hung up, I began calling each of the providers who'd agreed to help with Amelia's service.

The previous week, as Amelia's case had unfolded in the news, I'd been contacted by an organization called Little Angel Gowns. Curious, I peeked at their website, which explains,

> We work with hospital bereavement programs to provide burial gowns and pouches to grieving families. These gowns and pouches are made from wedding dresses, formal dresses and first communion dresses. We are funded solely by donations and work on a volunteer basis. Each gown is individually wrapped in tissue and presented to families by the medical team caring for their baby.

Yes, I replied to their Facebook message, *prepare me a gown!*

Now, just days later, I was calling everyone back—Little Angel Gowns, Indiana Funeral Care, Washington Park Cemetery—asking if their efforts could be doubled. I knew that each request generated either administration and paperwork or physical labor. Sometimes all three. The answers I received, though, were a resounding chorus of yeses.

Both babies were picked up from the coroner's office on Tuesday, January 13, to be prepared for a double ceremony on Saturday.

BODYGUARD NEEDED

Steve had just left the country to pastor the staff at Mission to Ukraine and I was missing his steadfast support. I felt a bit anxious about hosting this double funeral in his absence. Both of the babies had lost their lives under suspicious circumstances and I wondered who might show up. I couldn't predict what might happen at the burial. I would have loved to have had Steve at my side. But I knew that I had his blessing and sensed a strong affirmation from the Lord that pointed to a double funeral for these girls.

Mid morning the previous Friday, my friend Cindy had brought two women over to my home. She'd told me a few weeks earlier that they'd recently named their babies who'd been aborted years earlier, and I'd had charms made for them. That morning I gave them the charms inscribed with the names of the children they'd lost, and the four of us prayed together.

Before they all left, I shared a bit about the upcoming service and my disappointment that Steve would be absent. "What I really need is a bodyguard," I quipped. Without missing a beat, Cindy offered her son Sam, who'd recently turned nineteen. I was certain it wasn't an assignment he'd asked for or been prepared for, but I accepted nonetheless.

Tuesday night, the Lord woke me at 2:30 a.m., prompting me to go downstairs and read the paperwork the coroner's office had faxed. I'd already read over it, but obediently trod downstairs to take a quick glance. I opened the file folder where I'd put the document and noticed something I'd not seen before. The standardized form I'd seen on so many occasions authorized permission for burial or cremation of the body. But Geraldine and her advocate had altered the form. "Burial" had been whited out, and so the box that had been checked read only, "Permission to cremate."

This mattered.

The next day I called Sharon, Geraldine Green's social worker, to learn more. She arranged for me to call Geraldine on Thursday morning.

Geraldine explained to me that when she was to be released, in March 2016, she wanted to be able to come and pick up the remains of her daughter. Of course, I reasoned, Indiana had never been her home; Illinois was. Geraldine also instructed me to house the remains in a Minnie Mouse urn. That request proved to be more difficult than cremation.

I agreed to cremate Harmoni's body and asked Geraldine's permission to host a service in her daughter's honor. She agreed. I told her about the beautiful gown I'd received the day before and asked if she'd like me to keep it for her following the service.

"No," she said. "Cremate her in it."

Then, wistfully, she added, "It's all I'll have of her."

GOWNS REVEALED

As the media continued to follow the unfolding story of Amelia, I was invited by a local journalist to be a guest on her morning show.

When I walked into the TV station on Thursday afternoon to film the segment for the next morning, I had a very special package tucked under my arm. At the end of our conversation I invited viewers to join us on Saturday morning at eleven for the service and I unwrapped two precious custom gowns, which I'd just picked up from Little Angel Gowns. They were embroidered with winding ivory vines laced with pearls and satin flowers. They were perfect.

After the taping, when I returned to my car, I checked a weather report and discovered that freezing rain was expected on Saturday. Before I pulled away from the TV station I called the cemetery director to ask what our options might be. We'd always done graveside services but, in this case, that just didn't seem feasible. Unfazed, he suggested we use the cemetery's Mount Vernon Chapel.

Before going home, I drove to the cemetery to lay eyes on the chapel. Though humble on the outside, the interior was cream-colored marble from floor to ceiling. Large oriental rugs lay in the foyer and entry. The long narrow room, with no center aisle, was filled with twenty rows of wooden pews. The side walls and front featured high stained glass windows. Because there was no pulpit or table up front, the director and I dragged a matching set of drawers, tucked away in a side alcove, to the front of the chapel and covered them with linens we also found.

The next morning, when I returned to the chapel at ten, people had already begun to gather. As instructed by his mother, nineteen-year-old Sam had arrived early, dressed in his Sunday best, ready to be my bodyguard. He looked and behaved like he could be in the Secret Service.

I'd been expecting to meet Nichole at the chapel, and looked for her there, but she'd not yet arrived.

The rarely used chapel had been cleaned and was ready for those who would come to pay their respects. I positioned the flowers and arranged a stand for my notebook.

At ten minutes after ten my phone rang, and I recognized Nichole's number.

"I overslept and missed the bus," she explained.

Firmly, I instructed, "I need you to get here."

Nichole had been such an important part of other services we'd conducted, and I wanted her to be a part of this one.

While Marian and I made last-minute touchups to the chapel, a woman I'd never met came up to me and shared her story. Pearl was about forty-five, and the mother of three. She'd seen the news story and had come to show her support. "I lost a baby," Pearl explained to me. "My community was amazing. They supported me and got me through it." She continued, "I didn't want this baby to be alone."

I thanked Pearl for her tender heart and continued preparing for the service.

A few minutes later, another woman, in her thirties, quietly approached me. Turning from my binder of notes, I said hello and she introduced herself as Ashley.

"When I was new to Indianapolis," Ashley explained, "I gave birth to a stillborn baby. I hadn't met anyone in town yet, and felt so alone. I had no one." Unhealed pain washed over her face. As Pearl had just done, Ashley also said, "I didn't want this baby to be alone."

Isn't that amazing? God was using each of these women to honor the lives of two precious baby girls.

Marian, wearing a deep purple suit jacket and black slacks, was standing nearby when a third woman approached me. This well-dressed, middle-aged stranger simply announced, "I want to make a donation."

Although I'd never gone looking for money to support the ministry,

God had guided me to accept all offers of donations. It was an important way that people could participate. I thanked the woman and let her know the easiest way to contribute.

When she walked away, Marian shuffled up beside me, whispering in my ear, "Do you know who that is?"

"No," I answered, "should I?"

"It's Mrs. Crane," Marian explained, "from the Crane murders."

I'd seen the story on the news. The Cranes' twenty-one-year-old son had been murdered by a group of friends in a dispute over a video game. Their granddaughter had also been caught in the fray and had been killed as well.

After Marian filled me in, I approached Mrs. Crane.

"I think you're so brave to be here," I told her. "Can I ask what brings you here today?"

Somber, lips pressed together, she released them to offer, "Today my son would have been twenty-five." I told her I couldn't think of a better way to honor his memory than by honoring the lives of Amelia and Harmoni.

I thanked her and prayed with her. As ten thirty approached, I dashed back to the cemetery office to meet the singer.

I'd just greeted him when Nichole came flying in the door.

"How'd you get here?" I asked, curious.

Talking a mile a minute, she explained, "I knocked on every door in my apartment building until I found someone awake. I told them I'd pay them ten dollars to drive me here."

Clever, I mused.

Without pausing to catch her breath, she asked, "So, do you have ten dollars?"

I didn't. I asked Marian and she didn't.

Sam, sweet nineteen-year-old stand-up Sam, pulled ten dollars out of his wallet.

I could see the cars beginning to line up outside, and instructed Sam to run out and give it to the driver of the car, and to get him out of there so the traffic could move through.

We got into the vehicles waiting at the front of the line and processed slowly toward the chapel. The hearse I rode in was the first to reach the gate in front of the chapel. As I stepped out, I turned my head to see that cars just kept coming and coming. There was nowhere to park, and the width of the road only allowed for one car. So we simply stopped.

In the back of the hearse, the kind shaped like a minivan, Amelia's and Harmoni's small caskets had been secured. Harmoni's was a standard size for a one-year-old and Amelia's was not much bigger than a box I might receive in the mail with a pair of boots.

When we stepped out, funeral director David Ring asked me, "You'll carry Amelia, right?"

I hadn't thought about it until that moment, but I heard "Yes" come out of my mouth.

Turning to Sam, I instructed him to carry Harmoni's casket, telling him, "You'll never be the same afterward." Since Harmoni was larger, Sam and Chris Wilburn, the police officer who'd sung at Nicholas's service and who would now be singing for Amelia and Harmoni's, carried it together.

As I lifted the box holding tiny, precious Amelia, I suddenly realized, "Wow, she's really in here." So many of our rituals around death—embalming the body, perfecting hair and makeup, selecting fine garments, and even the pristine casket—keep a bit of death's sting at bay. Suddenly, though, I was keenly aware that I was carrying a lifeless human body.

A group of us processed up a set of marble stairs to the chapel. We entered the rear of the chapel and processed forward, down opposite side aisles. At the front I laid Amelia's casket on one makeshift table and the guys rested Harmoni's on the other. As I turned to see the crowd, it was an incredible moment.

Stalwart supporters Nichole and Addy were there.

I saw my nephew, Christian, in the back of the chapel with his wife and kids.

I saw Jerry Junior with both of his parents.

I saw Mrs. Crane.

I noticed as the woman who'd delivered a stillborn baby wiped away a tear.

SERVICE

I greeted everyone in the name of Jesus and shared what I'd seen earlier that morning with the eyes of my heart.

I'd woken early and worshipped in our bedroom. Then, scrolling up my Roman shade I saw that the eastern sky was glowing bright pink. Unexpectedly, I was overcome with holy laughter. The Indiana Colts would be playing later in the day for a spot in the play-offs. Indianapolis had been blue-crazed all week leading up to the game. The brilliant burst of a bright pink sky on the morning of the girls' service was as if God was smiling and celebrating these precious young lives along with us. God's unmistakable writing in the heavens was so glorious that even the impressive and vibrant display of Colts-blue paled in comparison!

When the service began it was standing-room only as 120 people packed into Mount Vernon Chapel. Though I recognized the folks from my community, most of the people in the crowd were strangers to me.

Nichole, now integral to so much of He Knows Your Name's ministry, read Scripture, Marian offered a prayer for women struggling with infertility, and Reverend Manifold prayed for the babies' mothers as he'd done in the service for Baby Moses. After the ceremony we drove to the graveside. The ground was muddy. Sam, dutiful, held my boots as I slipped out of my shoes.

At the graveside, Tim Bray's mother, Addy, lit and held two red candles, holding them as I performed the brief graveside committal service. When Chris Wilburn sang "Jesus Loves Me," everyone joined in. I read Scripture and shared the gospel. In one of the two flower bouquets that had been set out, donated by a friend who'd experienced infant loss, a bright pink Gerbera daisy caught my eye. I dropped it into Amelia's grave, and other mourners followed suit.

At the end of the service, Chris sang one of the songs that had become a favorite among the growing He Knows Your Name family: "Lullaby and Goodnight."

It was hard to find a dry eye in the crowd.

Amelia, without any known kin, had been so utterly alone in the world. Held in my heart, I adopted her in death the way I'd adopted Moses Prince. Following the funeral, I thanked everyone who'd participated and, before she could slip away, I approached Jessica who'd so tenderly handled Amelia's body. I pulled a small box from my pocket and offered her a charm necklace to honor her and her work with baby Amelia.

Gathering my things, I offered Nichole a ride to her apartment. We were both hungry and stopped for a bite of lunch on the way. After we ordered, I got a phone call from Indiana Funeral Care, letting me know they were ready to cremate Harmoni's body.

"Wait, what?" I balked.

Although Geraldine Green had made it very clear that this was her wish, I wasn't ready for it.

"Alright," I agreed, "you can do it. Cremate her and then catalog it. I want to make sure this mom can find her daughter."

As I hung up the phone, I wondered briefly whether the mother of Amelia Grace Hope had been following the news coverage of the service. My wish for her was the same as it was for Geraldine: that both would find their daughters—in the arms of the Father who loved their babies and who loved them.

God was showing me how his plans to engage others with his mission in the world went well beyond anything I could orchestrate. Jessica had chosen Amelia's middle name. Little Angel Gowns, Indiana Funeral Care, and Washington Park Cemetery were all giving generously. I was seeing my friend Cindy reaching out to care for other grieving mothers. Pearl, who'd lost a baby of her own, wanted to support Amelia and Harmoni as she'd been supported. Ashley, who'd been alone in her loss, also wanted to lend her support. Mrs. Crane was honoring her son's memory. Nichole and Addy had come to confirm the value of the young lives lost. Nineteen-year-old Sam was serving. Chris Wilburn was lending his voice to the services. The gifts of each willing servant stood as a vivid reminder that this ministry was God's, not mine.

CHAPTER 13

Waking from a
Childhood Nightmare

*A*fter seeing a clip in the news about He Knows Your Name, a woman emailed me, having caught a glimmer of hope of redemption for the first time in decades.

"My name is Ellie Murphy. Please let me tell you my story. It's really my husband's story, and he does not know I'm writing this to you."

She explained that for almost half a century Chuck had lived with guilt about the death of his younger brother when Chuck was just four years old. Though part of him knew that he was not responsible, another part had carried that guilt for decades. Ellie explained that he often visited his brother, Billy, at the cemetery. Chuck also had a sister who'd been stillborn, buried two graves away from Billy. Her name was Emma. Without headstones, Chuck had trouble finding his siblings. He knew the general area where they were buried, but never knew exactly where.

Ellie's email explained:

> He goes there anyway and spends time in silence with them. I have been married to Chuck for almost 21 years. I know person-ally and deeply that his greatest regret is that he was never able

to have enough money to buy a headstone for his little brother.
He feels this way about his sister too but he never knew her.

Ellie had perceived the depth and meaning of Chuck's connection
to his siblings. Typically, when a young one is lost to miscarriage or
stillbirth or other infant loss, the impact he or she has had on those
around them is tragically minimized. People often assume that because
these lives were cut short before they could blossom into what they were
meant to be, they had little or no effect on those around them. Chuck's
experience also exposed the myth that a life's value and impact could be
measured in days or months or years.

Ellie continued her email:

> Chuck is on disability. There is no way he will ever be able to
> afford to put a stone there for his brother. There is no one else
> that goes to visit Billy's grave but Chuck, even though both par-
> ents are still living. It would be so wonderful for my husband
> to know that once he is gone from this world that Billy will be
> marked that he was once on this earth, that his little life mat-
> tered, at least to Chuck!

His little life mattered.

Her email ended, "Please, can you help?"

My heart raced with the conviction that this—setting his beloved
children free from the enduring weight of guilt and sin and death, in
this life and the next—is exactly what God longed to do in broken hearts.
Chuck's heart, his marriage, and his family begged for God's gracious
healing touch to take root.

Pausing to close my eyes and pray, I recognized God's familiar green
light.

THE LINGERING MEMORY

When Ellie and I connected personally, she described more of the piv-
otal day that had haunted her husband for decades.

Through trial and error, four-year-old Chuck had learned that when he tolerated his stepmother's abuse, she wouldn't touch his two-year-old brother, Billy. Vicky Murphy, the bully who was new to their home, would rage, threaten, push, kick, hit, and twist. In the mind of a desperate four-year-old, suffering her blows was the only way he knew how to protect his younger brother.

Day after day, he did.

One day in June of 1970, Chuck's father had left home at six o'clock to catch a bus to his shift at the Chrysler factory. As the boys played in the front yard, Billy was pushing a toy car around the porch and Chuck was tucked beside a bush, drawing in the dirt with a stick. Vicky, clutching her morning "coffee" that smelled nothing like coffee, was swinging on the front porch swing.

That morning Chuck was just out of eyesight.

"You better not be getting dirty," she threatened.

Chuck remained silent. Glancing down, Chuck noticed for the first time that the knees of his pants were soiled with ground-in dirt.

Vicky must have realized the same, because she hissed, "Let me see you, you little . . ."

Chuck froze. He didn't know what to do. If she beat him for no reason, he couldn't imagine what she'd do now that he'd given her what he perceived as legitimate reason to do it. Chuck heard the rhythmic creaking of the porch swing slow and then stop. His heart raced.

"Don't make me get you, boy," she hissed.

Chuck knew that if she had to stand up and come to him, his punishment would be doubled. Terrified, though, he remained frozen. But when Vicky stood to find him, he ran for his life, ducking down the driveway, dipping through bushes, and pressing his body behind a neighbor's garage. After chasing him down the driveway, stumbling and cursing, Chuck's stepmother gave up. She continued to rant, her voice trailing off as she returned to the front porch.

As he began to breathe again, Chuck thought of Billy. Chuck had been the one to make his stepmother so angry, and he was worried about what she might do to Billy. Sneaking home, Chuck slipped inside a low kitchen cabinet and pulled the door toward himself. Leaving the door open a crack, Chuck could hear and see the front porch.

Billy was still playing with his toy car. When he pushed it down a grooved floorboard, past Vicky, she kicked Billy as hard as Chuck had ever seen. Little Billy went sprawling, hitting his head on the floor. He burst into tears and Vicky ignored his cries. Eventually he began playing again.

When Billy pushed his car to the far side of the porch, Vicky summoned, "Billy, come here."

Chuck, still hidden, stopped breathing for a moment.

When Billy toddled over to her, Vicky kicked him again. This time he was propelled across the porch and Chuck could hear his head hit the brick pillar.

Vicky ignored his cries.

From his hiding place, Chuck watched this horrible cycle continue until Billy no longer stood up.

In the days and years that followed, per Vicky's story, everyone else would believe his death, attributed to a freak head injury from an "accidental" fall, to be a tragic accident. Chuck, though, knew that he'd seen his brother murdered.

That Chuck still carried a burden of guilt—for what no four-year-old should ever have to carry—resonated with the experience of others I'd walked with who'd also lost loved ones. Even when there's nothing a mother or father, sibling or grandmother, could have done differently to save a life, many are still haunted by what-ifs. What if I'd protected him? What if I'd driven her to school? What if I'd done something differently when I was pregnant? It was a senseless burden I knew God longed to lift.

DOUBLE SURPRISE

When Ellie contacted me on her husband's behalf, she'd offered her yes in response to God's deep desire to set Chuck free. My yes quickly followed. Ellie and I began to conspire about headstones both for Billy and for Emma. As we discussed how they should read—"Bill" or "Billy," "Emily," as cemetery records showed, or "Emma," the way Chuck had always understood his sister's name—we decided that what mattered most is that the wording and image be meaningful to Chuck: Billy and Emma.

When Ellie let Chuck know what we'd been up to, he was overwhelmed. Ellie reported, "I haven't seen him this touched and joy-stricken ever!"

As Ellie and I worked on the headstones, I discovered that when she and Chuck were newly married, living in Arizona, she delivered a baby who was stillborn. Although it seems absurd, the hospital had discouraged fathers from being in the delivery room, especially when there would be a death.

As Ellie labored to deliver the child she knew had died, the nurse asked, "Do you want him to come back? Because he doesn't have to come back."

Her tone suggested that it would be more kind to spare him the burden. So Ellie said she didn't want him there. Out of care for her husband, Ellie thought it would be better if he didn't witness the birth of his dead daughter because she believed it would be too hard on him. Honoring the request, the nurse prohibited Chuck from coming to be with his wife. Over the years, Ellie explained, this had been a sore spot in their marriage. Chuck would have loved to have been there to support her, but had been prohibited. And that had compounded his grief.

Although heartbreaking, I was touched that each had wanted to care for the other.

Gently, I asked Ellie, "Where is your baby?"

"I have no idea," she answered. "I think they put her out with the trash."

My heart hurt when I heard it.

Her baby hadn't been born in the 1940s or 1950s. It had been 1995! Chuck's sister had been born thirty years earlier. Yet her body had been kept; she had been named and she had been buried. I couldn't fathom a hospital culture that would operate as the one in Phoenix had.

Curious, I asked, "Did you ever name her?"

Naming was such an important part of the healing process for so many parents who have endured early infant loss.

"I did," Ellie shared. "I named her Jessica, and Chuck has always referred to her as Jessica Love."

Of Hebrew origin, the name Ellie had chosen for her daughter means "God beholds." As I considered the generations of pain in Chuck's family that had been systematically disguised and ignored, the name seemed divinely inspired. There is no death, no abuse, no agony that God does not behold and grieve. The trauma that Chuck had borne for so many years was also known and held by the Father who does not fail. Ellie's care was an incarnate expression of God's own noticing, remembering, grieving, caring.

As if Jessica Love's name needed an explanation, Ellie added with a chuckle, "We were kind of hippies and we gave her a flower child name!"

Ellie told me how redemptive it was to be working with me to provide these headstones for Chuck's siblings as a way to offer a salve for her husband's deep grief, especially because—in the loss of Jessica Love—she felt as though she'd added to his pain. From my end, it was such a holy privilege to watch the dynamic between Chuck and Ellie. What they were experiencing together was profound and very beautiful to behold. They worked together to choose the artwork for the two headstones. Chuck chose a Big Wheel, a plastic riding toy popular in the 1970s, for Billy, and a triskele design, three interlocking spirals, for Emma. Billy's headstone identified him as "Brother," and Emma's identified her as "Sister."

DEDICATION

When the headstones were set, I stood beside them with Chuck, Ellie, their children, and their children's spouses. Chuck and Ellie's first grandchild, just one month old, slept snuggled in her car seat. They'd all wanted to be a part of the dedication.

There was no question in my mind that Billy's and Emma's headstones would facilitate Chuck's healing process. I also knew God longed to release him entirely from the heavy yoke he'd been carrying. When we prayed together graveside, I asked Chuck to surrender his pain, his blame, his guilt.

With tears in his eyes, he did.

When we released balloons during the dedication, Chuck released a black one. As he let it go, he announced with authority, "It is finished."

God had finished it. In a twenty-first-century triumph of life over death, resonating deeply with the Easter story, I saw the gospel come alive once again beside a grave. Chuck's heart was at last free. After we'd prayed and released so much more than helium-filled latex to the heavens, I offered Ellie a charm engraved "Jessica Love."

As the couple remembered her together, Chuck offered, to me, "She apologizes to me every day for losing the baby."

For twenty years Ellie had suffered under the same twisty evil logic her husband had been duped by for forty-five years. The lie that insists there was something that she could have done differently to sustain the baby's life or to care for her husband. That there was something she had failed to do. That there was something she was "guilty" of.

As Chuck examined the charm hanging from Ellie's neck, he reassured her, "You don't ever have to say 'I'm sorry' again."

With his encouragement, beside the grave, Ellie also released what was not hers to bear.

As the two embraced one another, the eyes of my heart could see God's healing grace washing over them.

HORIZONTAL AND VERTICAL HEALING

I loved that all of Chuck and Ellie's children had been present that day. In too many families, brokenness has been passed down from generation to generation. Beside Billy's and Emma's graves, God was healing the entire Murphy family. When Ellie reached out to care for her husband, his heart shifted; when he relieved her of the need to repeat an ineffective "I'm sorry," hers shifted. Psychologists refer to this kind of dynamic as "family systems." When one person in the system gets healthy, the entire dynamic shifts and others often experience transformation and redemption as well.

And just as God was healing the Murphy family horizontally, he was also redeeming it vertically. With the eyes of my spirit I can see that the ripples of healing released by God that day are already moving through the spirit of a one-month-old baby girl. That child will grow up stronger and healthier because of the brave, hard, prayerful redemption that Chuck and Ellie allowed God to do.

As I drove from the cemetery back to my home, I was overwhelmed by what I had seen of God's graciousness. It was a lesson I'd tuck away and return to again: in the most impossible situations, where families have long ago lost hope that restoration is possible, God is still in the business of healing human hearts. There is no hurt that is outside of God's view and God's power.

Truly, God beholds.

Just as I might have shut off the evening news and quickly forgotten about a baby who'd been found in a dumpster, Ellie didn't *have* to contact me on behalf of her husband. She might also have found my story interesting, shut off the TV, and missed an opportunity to partner in God's gracious redemption. But her single step of faithfulness, responding to an internal nudge to action by sending an email, had triggered the graciously ordained events that unleashed healing in her husband's heart and throughout their family.

In many ways it appeared that, with the exception of his wife's support, Chuck Murphy had been alone in his suffering for decades. He was the only person to know the truth about his brother's death. He'd never had the opportunity to know his sister or daughter. Others likely disregarded his losses as negligible. But thanks to the tender care of his wife, Chuck at last had the opportunity to heal and to grieve. Though some might call Ellie's response to the news story "coincidental," I'm convinced that God had always held Chuck's grief close to his heart and longed to breathe his healing into Chuck's life. By stepping out to care for her husband, Ellie opened the doors for God's healing.

It has always been my prayer that He Knows Your Name would become unnecessary as Christ's body cares for its members who are hurting and need healing. I'd seen my friend Cindy engage as she ministered to women who'd endured abortions. I'd watched as Marian at Washington Park East Cemetery cared for families whose hearts were still throbbing with pain. And I'd just seen Ellie usher in God's healing through her tender care for her husband. Spirit-driven acts of love like these can be as simple as bringing a casserole to a grieving colleague or praying with a friend after a miscarriage. Entering in might involve traveling to celebrate a life worth honoring or raising money for a local family to bury a loved one. God was showing me, through Ellie and others, that all he needs from any one of us is one small yes.

CHAPTER 14

The Joys and Trials
of Saint Tamia

W hen a young life is lost, we naturally imagine what might have developed in the person we've been privileged to glimpse for a short season. How would Jessica Love have loved others? What would Dominique have accomplished after graduating from college? In what ways would Tim have continued to impact and bless his Indianapolis neighborhood? How might young Annaliese's prayer ministry have exploded? We grieve what we did know of a loved one and we also mourn what we will never be able to know.

When I ripped open and unfolded an eight-page letter I received from a Louisiana woman, I began to discover that the immeasurable value and impact of any given human life does not ever depend on what an individual is expected to accomplish. All that matters is that he or she reflects the image of God. Even when an individual's future appears dim in our eyes, simply bearing the image of God is enough.

Tamia Trufant-Wade, whom I've come to think of as Saint Tamia of New Orleans, taught me that.

SPARK OF HOPE

"I'm writing about a need for help with a headstone for my foster son, Tremon."

When Tamia finally found a moment in her full schedule to watch her DVRd episodes of the *Steve Harvey* show, she'd seen the story of the Finney children. Like the twinkle of possibility Ellie had glimpsed on the Indianapolis evening news, the show sparked a possibility for Tamia as well.

After he was born just outside of New Orleans, Tamia explained, her foster son Tremon spent the better part of his first eighteen months in the hospital on a ventilator, twenty-four hours a day. Cerebral palsy meant his muscles were weak. Tremon had also been born with Down syndrome and pulmonary hypertension.

During those months, Tremon's social worker, Sarah Smith, searched for a family to receive him. It wasn't easy to place healthy children, and finding a home for a child with special needs was riddled with complications. Whoever accepted Tremon would have to be specially trained to manage the care of this fragile boy. Desperate, Sarah approached Tamia, who'd been trained as a therapeutic foster care mom. Over the previous decade Tamia had begun to welcome children with special needs into the home she shared with her husband, Steven. One had Down syndrome. Two used wheelchairs. Several had autism.

When Sarah approached Tamia, she didn't sugarcoat Tremon's needs. She couldn't. He would need around-the-clock supervision. After prayerfully weighing the needs of her family and discussing Tremon's condition with her husband, Tamia called Sarah and said she'd take Tremon.

HOMECOMING

For the fourteen days of intense training to learn about Tremon's care, Tamia lived at the Children's Hospital in New Orleans. She'd dash home for a shower or sneak out to go to church, but most of her hours were spent learning how to keep one sweet eighteen-month-old alive. She was trained in ventilation care and management of medication. She learned to use the complicated equipment Tremon needed, reading and interpreting the regular reports they produced.

Tremon joined Tamia, Steven, their two children by birth, and a handful of other foster children. Every day Tamia prayed that God would give her the ability to care for the fragile boy. She'd been told his lungs were so severely compromised that he would most likely never get off the ventilator. But when Tremon was three, Tamia began to wean him from the ventilator. Watching for signs of distress, she'd release him for increased periods of time. By the time he was four, Tamia's prayers had been answered. Tremon was at last able to be off the ventilator during the day, only depending on it at nighttime. This allowed him at last to crawl, using his arms like a US Marine, and to use a walker.

Tamia reports, "He loved to move! He loved to crawl over to the washer and dryer and listen to the vibration, patting them with his hand."

Yet as Tremon's health improved incrementally, Tamia's personal circumstances began to crumble.

FAMILY IN DISTRESS

Tamia's husband loaded trucks in a local warehouse. On February 22, 2012, Steven left for work at 4:45 a.m. as he typically did. Returning to the bedroom twenty minutes later, though, he sat down awkwardly on sleeping Tamia's feet. When she asked him what was going on, he was unable to speak. After Steven was transported to the hospital, doctors determined that he'd suffered a massive stroke. In the course of one odd morning, Tamia became full-time caregiver for one more person.

Five months after his stroke, as Steven continued to work at the recovery that included daily physical and occupational therapy, a mammogram detected three lumps in Tamia's breasts. Soon after, she was diagnosed with stage four breast cancer. With a rigorous treatment schedule, Tamia was forced to release the children in her home into temporary care. Tremon, of course, needed a very special placement. After another desperate search, Sarah found a temporary home for Tremon on the other side of the city.

Tremon was the child Tamia worried about the most during her illness. Over the years she'd learned to read his face for signs of distress. To listen to the rhythm of his breathing. To recognize in his eyes what he needed. While many people didn't understand how she could care for him, Tamia had never seen Tremon as a burden. Only a gift.

Tamia knew that if she was to get her children back, she had to first beat cancer. God was faithful to his faithful servant. Nine months after she'd been diagnosed, Tamia was declared cancer-free! Like a mother hen, Tamia began to gather all of her chicks back up under her wings.

Two weeks after returning home, though, Tamia was rushed to the hospital where an infection in her knee was drained and diagnosed as a strep infection. The infection was so severe that it required immediate surgery, and the children again had to be sent away. When Tamia was at last released, she was able to come home, attached to an IV pump for forty-two days, and finally beat the infection. With her doctor's okay, Tamia set her heart again on gathering her children.

The first one to come home was seven-year-old Dequinn. Legally blind, wheelchair-bound Dequinn depended on Tamia for every activity of daily living. The next day, seven-year-old Sean came home. Sean was more able physically, but needed constant supervision.

The process of bringing Tremon home needed a little more care. Because he'd already endured several confusing transitions, Sarah and others charged with his care wanted to ease his return home. Tamia's first step was to request permission to schedule visits with Tremon in her home. The plan was that she would pick him up in the afternoon, have him over for dinner, and return him to his current foster home before bedtime. Eventually, as he became comfortable there again, he'd move home for good.

The first visit was scheduled for a Saturday. After she got Steven's breakfast Friday morning, Tamia began to scurry around the home, straightening it up, the way an expectant mother who was "nesting" might do. Excited to have her baby back, she wanted everything to be in order for Tremon's visit. When the phone rang at ten thirty, she recognized Sarah's number. She was probably calling, Tamia reasoned, to confirm the time of the next day's visit.

But that's not why Sarah had called.

"Tamia," Sarah said, weakly, "this is Sarah."

Her voice wavered, as if fighting back emotion.

"I thought you might call," Tamia bubbled. "I'm all ready for tomorrow."

"It's not that," Sarah replied.

Sarah explained that the previous evening, Tremon's temporary foster mother had put him down in his bed for the night. He'd had cold symptoms throughout the day. She'd made sure he was comfortable and hooked him up to the ventilator. After tucking in her other children, she'd gone to bed.

Friday morning when she returned to his room, Tremon, just four months from celebrating his fifth birthday, had died from respiratory failure.

Tamia couldn't believe what she was hearing. She struggled to process what Sarah was saying.

A week later, Tamia's family gathered to bury Tremon, a boy she'd loved as if she'd given birth to him.

A MOMENT OF REST

Still caring for three children and her husband in her home, Tamia didn't have much margin for relaxation in her life. But when she did, she treated herself to a few episodes of *Steve Harvey*. When I mentioned that He Knows Your Name had provided a headstone for Renee Finney, really for her children, Tamia began to weep.

Then, in faith, she looked up into the heavens and thanked God.

Three days later, I received the bulky letter from Tamia, explaining that Tremon had been buried in a rural cemetery between Baton Rouge and New Orleans. Though the state had covered the burial expenses, they had not purchased a headstone. Tamia would have loved to provide one, but was strapped financially.

Tamia wrote me to ask if He Knows Your Name might provide a headstone for Tremon. The more I read, the more right it seemed.

Tamia's eight-page appeal was neatly written on lined notebook paper. Her request was polite, kind, generous. Honoring Tremon's birth mother, she explained, "It will not only be greatly appreciated by my family but will as well by his biological mother and her family." Tamia had always welcomed Tremon's biological mother to spend time with him in Tamia's home. His face was round, like hers, and he had her beautiful dark, round eyes.

Tamia didn't blame Tremon's temporary foster mom for his death at all. Tamia understood that she'd done everything she could. Sadly, Tamia blamed herself. In the letter she reasoned, "If I hadn't asked that he stay at the other foster home until I was completely healed, then just maybe I would have known something was going wrong with his breathing and he would still be here with us." She was tangled up in the tricky deception of what-ifs.

My heart ached as I read her letter.

When I called Tamia to let her know I'd love to provide a headstone for Tremon, she immediately became emotional. It's what she wanted so much for him.

Not only did I recognize God's leading to provide a headstone to honor the value of Tremon's life, I also prayed that it might facilitate healing in the hearts of three mothers who loved him: his biological mom, Tamia, and the foster mother who found his lifeless body. As we worked together on the wording and design for Tremon's headstone, I was touched by the way that Tamia honored and included Tremon's mother. With the eyes of my heart I could see Tremon's three mothers visiting his grave.

On what would have been Tremon's fifth birthday, two of those mothers stood by my side as we dedicated his headstone: Tamia and Tremon's biological mother. Tremon's first mother was ill and had been released from the hospital for just one day to attend. Her extended family, including Tremon's siblings, were there to support her. And, of course, Tamia and her whole family attended to honor the boy they loved.

Today, as we continue our friendship, Tamia's life is no less complicated than it was when Tremon was alive. The longer I know her, the more certain I am that I'm not worthy to be facedown in front of this saint. In fact, since meeting Tamia I've become convinced that on the day when the saints go marching in, Tamia—with Tremon by her side—will be leading the parade.

HIS LIFE MATTERED

Tremon's short life and death have paralleled a moment in our country's history when many voices are announcing that "Every life *matters*."

The most nuanced sentiment behind the rallying cry insists, "The life that has historically been neglected and diminished *matters*." Through Tamia, I witnessed the way in which a vulnerable life that most would overlook *mattered*. In fact, when I close my eyes I can hear God's voice joining a holy prophetic chorus:

> "The lives of folks who are under-resourced matter."
> "The lives of people with physical disabilities matter."
> "The lives of people with intellectual disabilities matter."
> "The lives of the most vulnerable among us matter."

To this day, Tremon's life reminds me often of the truly good news that *every life matters*.

Many of us will say that God loves everyone, but secretly believe that some lives—dynamic people with special gifts, those with the potential to accomplish great things—might be a little more precious than others. Tamia's steadfast, faithful love for Tremon is a beautiful picture of God's relentless passion for and commitment to even the most vulnerable among us. Through Tamia, God convinced me that Tremon's life was of inestimable value simply because he reflected God's image.

CHAPTER 15

The Terrible Person
They Say I Am

*I*n January of 2015, when I buried Amelia and Harmoni, the *Indianapolis Star* covered the funeral and suggested doing a story about He Knows Your Name. They wanted to cover the history and development of the organization Alfie had prophetically imagined years earlier. Though I probably wouldn't have chosen to have a reporter and photographer trail me for two weeks, it turned out to be a meaningful opportunity to pause and survey the previous six years.

One crisp, cold, January morning, writer Bobby King and photographer Kelly Wilkinson met me at Washington Park East Cemetery. As we meandered through Babyland, I paused at each headstone to share a bit about each child we'd laid to rest there.

As we left Zachary's grave, Kelly pulled out her camera and stood over his headstone.

"Hold on," I called out. "We need to wait a second. I've never let Zachary's headstone be photographed."

"Okay," she obliged. "I don't need to take that picture."

"Just a minute," I directed. "Can you back away for a minute?"

Dutifully, without asking why, she did.

I walked over to Zachary's headstone and paused there to listen. As my eyes fell on the headstone which read *Zachary Tibbetts* I asked the Lord, "Is it time?"

Zachary had been the first baby I'd buried, and I'd always chosen to be protective of this piece of Zachary's story because it included his mother's last name. All of the other headstones had either been abandoned children whom I had named or children named by their mothers who partnered with me to bury the children they'd lost.

As I looked at the carved letters of Zachary's last name, I was keenly aware of his first mother. She'd given him a first name and a last name. She and her family had known him and loved him for five months. He'd come into the world with a birth certificate, which she had, and he'd left it with an official death certificate, which I had. And though I'd worked to guard his identity from prying eyes, I had no interest in insisting on a rigid way if it wasn't God's way.

I'm keenly aware that the risk of "having an organization," crafting a tight mission statement, or printing a business card is that I'll begin to behave out of habit rather than moving in response to God's leading. I recognize the temptation and it scares me. The day that God stops guiding my steps—or rather the day I rush ahead of God without pausing to listen for his voice—is the day I want to be done.

But this was not that day. Five years earlier God had directed me to keep Zachary's headstone out of the public eye. How would God lead me today?

"Lord," I queried quietly in my spirit, "is it still supposed to be this way?"

I paused to listen.

It's time. It's been five years.

The six words were immediately impressed on my heart.

"Okay," I directed Kelly. "It's fine to photograph Zachary's headstone."

"Really," she protested kindly, "I don't have to do it."

"No," I assured her, "it's fine."

It would actually turn out to be more than fine.

FRONT-PAGE NEWS

Two weeks later Steve and I sat by the fire together enjoying a lazy morning because we had attended church Saturday evening, which was unusual for us. Around noon, having both lingered in our precious "hem time," allowing our spirits to be touched by the heart of Jesus as we paused in worship to touch the hem of his garment, we were feeling spiritually fed and physically hungry! Before we made lunch, I ran out for a Diet Coke. Since I was out, I decided to stop at the gas station to pick up the Sunday edition of the *Indianapolis Star.* The line at the cash register was long with people buying lottery tickets and cigarettes. I grabbed a paper, folded it in half, put it under my arm, then waited. When it was my turn, I handed the paper to the cashier. He unfolded it so he could swipe the barcode, and as he caught a glimpse of my blond hair he realized my picture was on the cover.

"That's you!" he exclaimed, looking down and then glancing back up at me.

I started to cry.

The cashier, biting down on a toothpick, was taken aback. He asked me if I was okay.

I nodded, took the paper back and refolded it. Slipping quickly out to my car, I cried all the way home. Back in the living room, still wet with tears, I handed it to Steve. He opened it and, without words, he teared up as he saw the color pictures from the double funeral displayed across the front page of the paper. Seeing Amelia's story given so much honor made my heart, and Steve's, so full. We were both surprised to find the story on the front page!

Though Kelly had photographed all of the headstones I'd shown her in Babyland, when we spread out the paper on the kitchen counter I saw that Zachary's was one of the few to have been included. It even seemed to pop off the page, and I had a sense that something more was going on than I could name in that moment.

INCOMPREHENSIBLE

When Alfie had first told me that no one had claimed baby Zachary from the morgue, I hadn't been able to make sense of what she was telling me. Zachary wasn't an anonymous baby the way Nicholas had once been, when he was known only as Baby Doe. Zachary's name was known. His mother's name was known. His grandmother's name was known.

Authorities knew where to find her. I struggled to understand why his family had not claimed his body.

And I'd also learned that Zachary's was not the only body to be unclaimed at the morgue. Abandonment is a reality coroners face more often than I want to know. And while part of me understood that, and even some of the reasons for it, I was gripped again by similar disbelief when Indianapolis's Eskenazi Health hospital ran an announcement in the paper that "Baby Harris" had been abandoned there. I learned from the hospital's Director of Bereavement that such announcements are standard protocol when bodies are not claimed by families. A jolt shot through my body as I realized that what happened to Zachary and others at the morgue also happened at *hospitals*. The incongruity between the boundless care offered to sick children in life was hard to reconcile with the same children being uncared for in death.

But seeing Zachary's headstone featured in the *Indianapolis Star* reminded me of the ways God had humbled my spirit and softened my heart since I'd buried Zachary. Over those five years I'd walked with enough desperate mothers to recognize that I'd never be fully able to stand in their shoes. God had expanded my heart for grieving parents by allowing me the precious privilege of walking with them. And God had used people like Nichole and Addy, Danyelle and Kelly, who had chosen to honor their children in death, to allow me to glimpse the incomprehensible suffering faced by those who had not.

When Kelly had innocently pointed her camera toward Zachary's headstone, God confirmed in my spirit that it was the right time for it to be photographed. And though I don't for a moment presume to understand God's unfathomable ways, I could recognize, in part, how it had taken five years to be the right timing for *me*.

And for someone else, as well.

PHOTO VERIFICATION

About a week after the article featuring He Knows Your Name was printed, I was working at my desk when I received a text from a dear friend, Susie. She'd attended various He Knows Your Name events through the years to remember and honor the lives of children she'd never met.

Though typically friendly and chatty, Susie simply instructed, "Send me a picture of Zachary's headstone."

She later told me she'd actually snapped a picture of Zachary's headstone years earlier, and had even hunted it down in her photo archives, but the glare from the sun had made Zachary's last name unreadable.

Curious, I agreed to send her one. Although I have several of my own pictures of the headstone in my archives, Sunday's paper was now sitting on my desk and so I snapped a shot and sent it to her. As it whooshed through cyberspace, I suddenly pieced together where Susie had been calling from. Every Friday morning she volunteers among homeless teen moms at Outreach Ministry. I hoped her abrupt message meant what I thought it meant.

An hour later Susie dialed me.

When I picked up, she offered simply, "You know why I'm calling."

I did.

"You found Felicia." I'd remembered Zachary's mother's name from the coroner's description of his visit with her and from seeing her name, five years earlier, on the release forms at the coroner's office.

She had.

"Yes. I just spent the morning with her and told her all about you and Zachary," Susie explained. "I've known her for quite a while and I just remembered that she had lost a baby boy about five months old, five years ago. When I read the paper on Sunday, something just clicked."

"How is she doing?" I asked hesitantly, remembering how overwhelming her life had been when Zachary had died.

"She is just getting her life back together," Susie shared. "She's eight months pregnant and has two other children. I asked her if she wanted to meet you and see his headstone." Susie paused, then continued, "I think it was a lot to process and she said that she didn't feel like she'd be ready next week, but would like to do it in two weeks."

GATHERING AROUND ZACHARY

Two weeks later, the three of us made plans to meet at the cemetery, along with two other women Felicia knew from the Outreach program. Knowing how emotionally taxing it could be, I'd been praying for Felicia throughout the week. When I pulled my car up to Babyland, with my daughter Caroline riding beside me, I could see Susie's car winding through the cemetery, making its way back to the baby section.

After they stopped, she and Felicia didn't get out of the car right away. Then Susie walked over to my window and explained that Felicia hadn't been prepared to see me with someone else. Susie had tried to explain to Felicia that it was my sweet daughter, but that only made her more anxious.

Sensitive to the situation, Caroline quickly offered, "Tell her I'll stay in the car."

Susie returned to her car and assured Felicia that Caroline wouldn't be involved.

I certainly related to Felicia's surprise at the sight of an extra person at such a tender juncture. I'd felt a similar anxiety, and I wasn't even the mom who'd lost a child.

Susie told me later that Felicia almost didn't come at all. The morning Susie was scheduled to pick her up, she'd wanted to sleep in and avoid the whole thing. When she finally exited Susie's car, and began walking to where I was waiting near Zachary's headstone, I recognized the apprehension on her face.

Felicia had brought a handwritten letter that she'd addressed to Zachary. It included two precious baby pictures of him and had been laminated. She also had a little photo album of pictures of him, as well as some white silk flowers.

After we'd been introduced to one another, about twenty feet from the grave, Felicia slowly approached Zachary's headstone.

Zachary Tibbetts
July 9, 2009–December 9, 2009
He Knows Your Name
Isaiah 56:5

When she read the words, she broke down weeping. The women from Outreach stood beside her and I hung back. After about five minutes, I approached.

"May I hug you?" I gently inquired.

Felicia answered bluntly, "No."

Her response reminded me that she didn't yet trust me. She had no reason to.

"That's fine," I assured her.

After a long silence, I thanked Felicia for her willingness to come and for allowing me to be there with her.

Appearing confused, she replied, "I am so thankful to you."

Curious, I asked Felicia, "How do you feel looking at this?"

Without hesitation, she answered, "I feel complete. I have wondered for five years where my son is. I guess it was just time that after five years I find him."

Her insight confirmed the word the Lord had given me about it being the right time to share the photo of her son's headstone publicly.

Felicia continued on to explain how hurt she was to have read in the papers that her son had been abandoned. In the years since Zachary's service I'd learned from Nichole and Addy and others how hurtful much of the media coverage could be to these grieving moms.

"I didn't abandon him," Felicia insisted.

Susie gently chimed in, "Sometimes people draw conclusions, based on our actions, that aren't true."

Memories of the awful things the media had assumed about the mother of Baby Doe found in a dumpster flashed through my mind. Sensational six o'clock sound bites could never capture the larger story of desperation and loss these mothers had endured.

Through tears and deep gasps, Felicia explained that there was nothing she could do. If she'd gone to the trustee's office seeking assistance, which is available in situations like this, she would have been required to prove residency as someone who pays property tax. Because she was homeless, she wasn't even able to access the slim funds available to bury her son. Everything I'd learned about the system of social services over the last several years confirmed all Felicia was saying.

As she gathered herself together, she told us that her son's name on his birth certificate was spelled "Zackery." I'd already learned this from Susie, who had mentioned it to me after meeting with Felicia. The error, knit somewhere into the bureaucratic paper trail which had produced his death certificate reading "Zachary" felt, to me, like another small indignity she'd been forced to endure. When I offered to have another headstone made with the correct spelling, Felicia said she'd think it over.

I could feel Felicia slowly relaxing a bit.

CHARM OF HONOR

Pulling a small, white jewelry box from my purse, I offered it to Felicia.

Lifting the lid, she saw the charm I'd had made for her. A silver silhouette of a boy read, "Zackery."

Over the years, I'd witnessed the significance for survivors of seeing the name of their loved one permanently etched in stone or in metal. I believe it's meaningful that God gave the law to Moses, on Mount Sinai, carved into stone. It was a lasting testament the people could see and touch. It lent legitimacy to Moses's report.

As I've accompanied families through grief, in both recent losses and those they've held in their hearts for decades, I've watched what happens when they see their loved one's name carved into a headstone. Adults who never knew a lost sibling display a visible awakening as they realize, "Oh, it's real. My parents weren't making up this story all these years. I had a sibling that I never knew. Now I know it's real." Parents like Felicia who've never had the opportunity to mark their children's graves experience the kind of completeness that Felicia described.

So when I give a mom a silver charm with her child's name engraved on it, it signifies the important lasting legacy of that child that will never fade from a mother's heart. Nichole and Addy and others have told me that everyone asks them about the charms they wear around their necks. It gives them an opportunity to share their story and keep the memory of their child alive. I believe those moments are healing salve for a mom's heart.

As I helped Felicia clip the chain around her neck, she said what I've heard from every other mother, "I'll never take it off."

With Zackery's name tucked near her heart, Felicia shared more of her personal story with us.

Susie asked if she could read Psalm 23 and then I prayed. On that cold day with snow spotting the ground, I thanked God for his white robe of righteousness that covers us. I asked that his Holy Spirit would warm and comfort Felicia as she continued to grieve the loss of her first-born son. I praised God for the purity of his love and his forgiveness that washes us and makes us white as snow.

When I finished praying, Felicia shared with me that, on the drive over with Susie, she'd decided at the last minute to stop at the dollar store to find another "something" for the grave. She said she didn't know why, but she selected the bunch of white flowers.

In response to my prayer about so many "white" things, she exclaimed, "Now that is God!"

NEVER FORGOTTEN

At Washington Park, the grassy area of Babyland butts up against a fence along a public sidewalk where the city bus stops. Three years after Zackery had been buried, Felicia would walk down that stretch of sidewalk every week to visit her daughter who was in foster care, just a block beyond Zackery's grave.

"Every time I walked along here," Felicia revealed, "I would always stop and turn and look. I never knew why."

I felt a chill pass through me.

Because all of the headstones in Babyland are flat, she never would have been able to see the names on them through the thick grass.

Pointing at Zackery's headstone, and then to the sidewalk just beyond the fence, she explained, "I'd get to there, stop, turn, and look. Then finish walking the rest of the block to go see my daughter."

Before she'd ever received her charm, Felicia had always carried Zackery close to her heart.

After I had buried Zackery, I assumed his story was done. What I've learned, from Felicia and from others, is that these stories, our stories, are never done. When one chapter closes, the story lives on through all those who have been touched by the life of a child. In every instance I see only part of a story that continues to unfold in ways I can't anticipate or imagine. That reveals God's redemptive heart to me. He unfolds his purposes like a flower, over time.

Five years earlier, I'd heard sparse bits of information about this mother who'd signed away rights to burying her son. At the time I hadn't understood. There was no way I could have. I saw only through my eyes, as any of us do, and it appeared to me that precious Zackery had been abandoned. This was how I'd referred to him, for years, when telling his story.

The day that changed for me, the day I began to speak of him differently, wasn't the day I learned about Felicia. It had actually been five weeks earlier when Bobby King and Kelly and I were exploring Babyland—just a few minutes before Kelly photographed Zackery's headstone. I recognize it when I watch the video of the story they produced. As I do, I notice that when I was telling Zackery's story, I didn't refer to him as being abandoned by his mother as I typically would have. Standing in front of his grave, I hadn't been able to get the word out. There's a pause in the recording where I am remembering the vulnerable mother who was without the resources to care for her son after death. I continued to say simply that his mother could not care for him.

As I retell stories, I don't want to get lazy and not rely on the Spirit to lead me. As audiences have invited me to share, I've retold many of these stories over and over. Yet as I become increasingly aware of the burden of brokenness in a grieving mother's heart, I continue to press into the heart of God to lead me. And now I was standing beside the very mother whose heart had been broken once by the loss of her son and, in smaller measure, again by the way his story had been told.

Before we said our good-byes and left the cemetery, I asked Felicia, "How would it make you feel for me to make a commitment to you that I will never again refer to him as being abandoned?"

Her face visibly relieved, Felicia confirmed, "That would mean a lot to me."

It was a promise I was glad to make.

When I returned to the cemetery several weeks later, I discovered that Felicia's letter to Zackery was still attached to his headstone. After weeks of freezing rain, I'd been surprised to find any remnant of it. Squatting down to read what she'd written above his sweet cherubic photo, the words that had flowed from Felicia's heart grabbed me: "I am not the terrible person that some people say I am." Felicia had given eloquent expression to what she, Nichole, Addy, and so many other mothers had experienced at the hands of media and public opinion. So I count it a kindness from the Lord that, by the most fortuitous and unlikely circumstances—springing from media coverage!—Felicia had finally been able to find and honor the son she'd loved. Her story wasn't over when we buried her Zackery, and I don't think it's over just yet, even now.

And neither is mine.

If you'd asked me six years ago if I loved God and was walking with him, I would have said, "Yes." Prayer, worship, and service were all woven into the fabric of my relationship with God. I received from God daily and I poured out into the lives of other women who were seeking God. And if you'd asked me whether every life mattered, I would have said, "Yes, of course." I believed in the sanctity of unborn lives. Steve and I championed Safe Families on behalf of vulnerable children. We supported ministries to those in need in Ukraine.

When you asked me if I loved God and loved people, I would have spoken an emphatic, *yes* and *yes*.

But in the most tumultuous season of my family's life, my *vertical* yes—loving God and serving him—collided with my *horizontal* yes—living as if every life mattered. That Spirit-fueled collision tore open the carefully stitched fabric of my life I was so desperately trying to hold together. In my darkest days, I could never have imagined that I'd discover my own healing and redemption amidst the suffering of others. Nothing about the route to redemption made sense.

If you'd felt my heart racing as I spoke to the coroner the first time, or knew how ill-equipped I felt standing before bereft mourners, it would be clear that I was walking in trepid obedience, not some divine magical bliss that made any of it easy. Nervously putting one foot in front of the other, I took one baby step: I made one phone call. For all I knew, that would be the end of it. But God invited me to take one more baby step. And then another. And then another.

It's probably best I couldn't see some of the places I'd end up as a result of those baby steps! Although I couldn't see clearly where I was headed, I was never alone. In every moment, every meeting, every conversation God had been present. He had gone before me, he had been with me, and he had been behind me. That assurance is what propelled me to step through every new doorway God opened. And without fail, God's comfort was being poured out into my heart as I shared it with others.

And that's exactly why I share my story.

The sacred place of suffering is the unlikely place where I found comfort and strength when I most needed it. And, in God's inscrutable economy, I've become convinced that it's where God longs to meet others as well. So I share my story in the hopes that one more person will notice God's gentle whisper. One more person will say a tentative yes. One more person will take one brave baby step into the unknown. One more person will taste life that really is life as they walk daily in response to God's leading.

I don't expect that anyone else's journey with God will look just like mine. God gives one person a passion for orphans. Another is called to free women and girls from human trafficking. Someone else will be moved to establish relationships at a local nursing home. Or in a prison.

I am confident of one thing: as you boldly step into the difficult places, God is faithful to use whatever you offer to accomplish his divine and holy will. So if you've sensed a nudge from the Holy Spirit, say *yes*.

I promise you that, in the most wonderful way, your life will never be the same.

ACKNOWLEDGMENTS

Steve, my love: Your heart is a deep well. No one says more yeses than you. Your yes for this book gave me the freedom to say yes because the timing was so challenging. Your tears of compassion and courage fan my flame for the kingdom work we share. Thank you for leading me by serving me, for nurturing my heart and giving me the honor of being the heart of our home. Worshipping Jesus with you in our marriage is my holy honor.

Lauren, Aram, Andrew, Heather, Rose Jubilee, Smith Moses, Anna, and Caroline: My mother's heart explodes with love for you. You have taught me how to love, how to be loved, and how to listen. You made me a mother, and I am eternally grateful for the sacred family life we share. You enrich my life with your tender hearts and bring me endless joy. I am so proud of each of you.

Eli: When you adopted me, you taught me more about love than my heart could handle at times. I love and adore you.

Jane, Tom, and Julie: It has been a divine privilege to carry the honor of Mom and Dad with you. They inspired us to dream, be generous, and treasure the gift of life. I love you.

My cup overflows with love and gratitude for each of you dear ones. When I received a dream from God instructing me to tell these stories, honestly, desire wasn't a partner of the dream. As I shared this journey with you, you celebrated the seed of possibility born in my heart. Thank you for carrying this dream with me and for the gift of encouragement you gave me to hope for the fulfillment of Revelation 21:5. Through you, desire was born. Together, we have said a collective yes.

Margot: Thank you for sharing your many gifts with me. You listened deeply and then carried my voice into this book with your craft in such a beautiful way. I have loved sharing He Knows Your Name with you. Thank you for stewarding the treasure of these lives with me. I'm thankful to Alice Crider for introducing us and for her confirmation that these special stories were indeed special!

Thank you to my Monday and Tuesday sisters and Life-giving friends. This book is the fruit of your faithful prayers. I have cherished your listening ears, love, and affirmation.

Thank you to the teams at Wordserve, Impact Author, and Kregel Publications for believing with me that every life matters. Thank you for your yeses and for teaching me how I could make this dream come to life.

I humbly thank my He Knows Your Name family and partners. You have changed me and inspired me. This book is your voice too. Together we have changed laws, brought healing, and seen miracles. Your friendships have completed me. I love you.

To Jesus, who is the great I am: This is all for you. I feel most satisfied in you when I stand graveside in complete assurance that life comes from the grave. It happens every time I minister in your name. Life. It's who you are. It's what you give. I humbly praise you for allowing me to hold your hand and walk this road. Oh gracious Savior, please keep inviting me; saying yes to you is my delight.

To all my precious adopted ones: Heaven will be glorious when we meet face-to-face. I long to hold you.

NOTES

1. Mother Teresa, *No Greater Love* (Novato, CA: New World Library, 2002), 120.
2. Debbie Taylor Williams, *Pray with Purpose, Live with Passion: How Praising God A to Z Will Transform Your Life* (West Monroe, LA: Howard Publications, 2006).
3. See www.operationtimothy.com.
4. Jerry Sittser, *A Grace Disguised* (Grand Rapids: Zondervan, 2004), 170.
5. Julie Gilchrist, MD. "Racial/Ethnic Disparities in Fatal Unintentional Drowning Among Persons Aged Less Than 29 Years." Centers for Disease Control and Prevention. May 16, 2014, www.cdc.gov/mmwr/pdf/wk/mm6319.pdf.
6. Sittser, *A Grace Disguised*, 49.
7. Cary Docter, "Racine Officials Seek Donations for Dead Baby's Headstone," June 11, 2013, http://fox6now.com/2013/06/11/racine-co-sheriffs-office-seeks-donations-for-dead-babys-headstone/.
8. Katie Davis, *Kisses from Katie: A Story of Relentless Love and Redemption* (New York: Howard Books, 2011), 91–92.
9. Henri Nouwen, *The Inner Voice of Love* (New York: Image Books, 1999), 51–52.

"The dignity of a proper burial, or a simple headstone to mark one's final resting place, may seem like a small thing to most people in Western society. But not to Linda Znachko. In *He Knows Your Name*, Linda recounts the deeply moving stories of desperate, often disadvantaged, parents who—on face value—seem to have failed their offspring in death as well as in life. But the story is never that simple, as Linda so compassionately narrates. Her journey of serving 'those who mourn' began with a first step of obedience in providing a proper grave for an infant abandoned in a dumpster. Her mission has since grown to include an ever-widening circle of caring individuals dedicated to the proposition that our very humanity consists in our ability to do the 'small things' well—to love and respect the least among us, whether in life or in death."

—CRISTÓBAL KRUSEN, chairman and CEO of Messenger Films, Inc.

"Linda Znachko could not have predicted how honoring one nameless, abandoned baby would lead to a vibrant celebration of life and love for otherwise rejected and forgotten people. By responding to God's prompting time after time, Znachko models a life of faith and obedience. The stories in her book remind us there is always more than meets the eye—and by opening our hearts, we can reach out without judgment and watch God bring healing."

—ANN KROEKER, writing coach and author of *The Contemplative Mom*, *Not So Fast*, and *On Being a Writer*

"'God's Spirit was prompting me to step into a stranger's deepest pain. Had I declined, no one around me would have been the wiser.' This quote stood out to me perhaps more than any other in Linda Znachko's anointed book, *He Knows Your Name*. Each of us has a choice to listen to the Lord's promptings or to decline. And, wow, what a journey the Lord will lead us on if we follow him! With its compelling prose and jaw-dropping, real-life stories guaranteed to bend even the most cynical person at the knees, if this book doesn't turn your ear toward what the Lord is doing and wants to do in the world, nothing will. Captivating, unbelievable, mesmerizing, and deeply profound, this book is a must-read for anyone looking for a miracle, for hope, and above all, for life."

—AMY K. SORRELLS, award-winning author of *Lead Me Home* and other novels of hope

"Linda Znachko's life calls all of us to care for 'the least of these.' She shares an incredible personal journey of giving love and dignity to those who have been passed by. It is not only a beautiful picture of Jesus's love for each one of us, but it is a powerful life lived for the sake of others. Her inspiration and story should cause all of us to pause and once again say yes to God's nudging of our heart to care for those who have no voice of their own."

—JIMMY SEIBERT, president of AMI Global Ministries